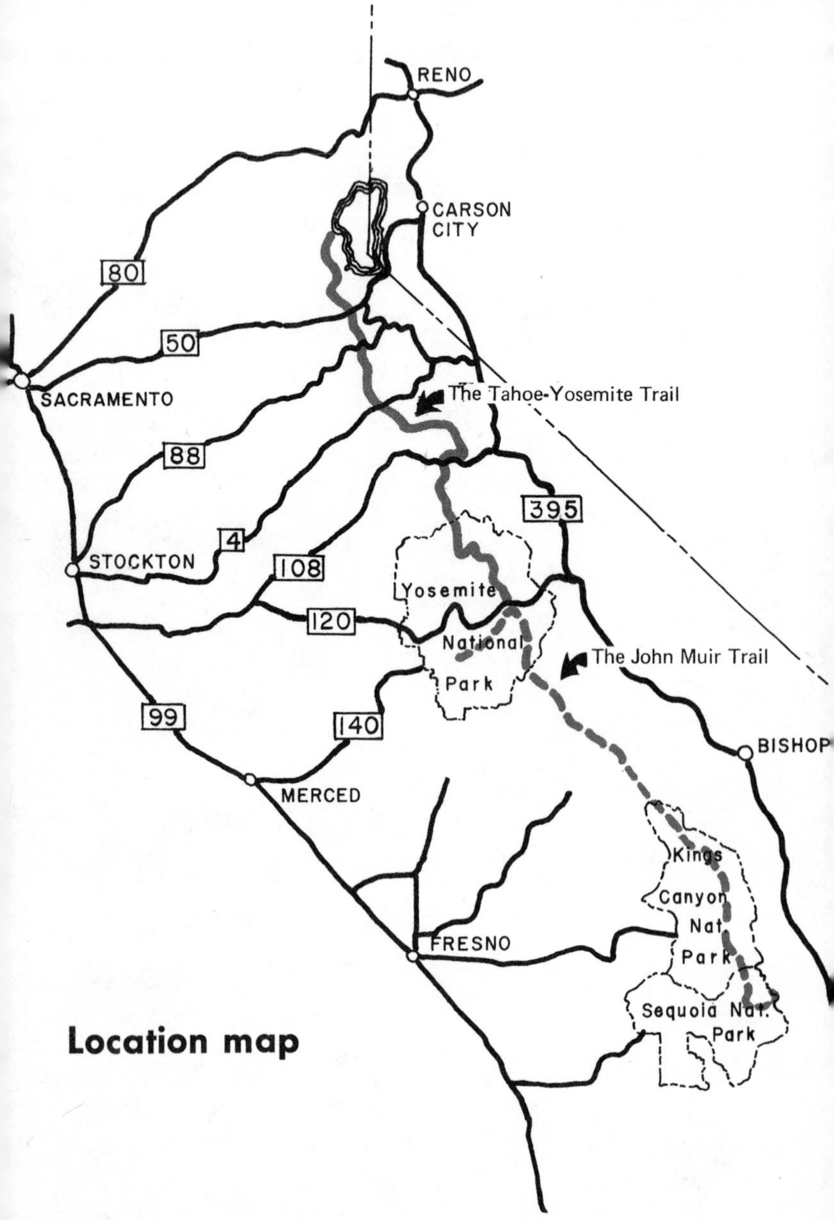

Location map

The TAHOE-YOSEMITE TRAIL

A comprehensive guide to the 180 miles of trail between Meeks Bay at Lake Tahoe and Yosemite Park's Tuolumne Meadows.

by

Thomas Winnett

Wilderness Press
BERKELEY

First printing May 1970
Second printing April 1971
Third printing June 1972
SECOND EDITION May 1975
Second printing February 1977
Third printing May 1978
THIRD EDITION June 1979

Photos by the author
(except as noted)
Design by the author

Field mapping by Jeffrey P. Schaffer, by Thomas Winnett (Winnemucca Lake to Highway 4) and by Ben Schifrin (Kennedy Meadow to Bond Pass and the Tilden Lake loop)

Maps drawn by Jeffrey P. Schaffer and Kenneth R. Ng

Library of Congress card number 78-65934
ISBN: 911824-76-6
Published by Wilderness Press
2440 Bancroft Way
Berkeley, CA 94704

TABLE OF CONTENTS

Tuolumne Meadows *National Park Service*

INTRODUCTION

The Forest Service first conceived the Tahoe-Yosemite Trail as early as 1914, but it does not exist officially even yet. We hope this book may help it become official.

Meanwhile, it exists in the mountains, the best place for trails to exist. Using this trail guide, one can with little difficulty follow its entire length of 180 miles from Meeks Bay to Tuolumne Meadows. The route is one that was chosen partly by the Forest Service, partly by the National Park Service, and partly by the authors. It passes through country far more varied than the country crossed by the more famous John Muir Trail, from the oak-and-maple-clad banks of the Mokelumne River at less than a mile elevation to the treeless, glaciated granite slabs of northern Yosemite two miles above sea level, from the "typical" Sierra gray granite of Emigrant Basin to the umber, sienna and slate volcanic battlements of Carson Pass.

Crossing four major highways, the Tahoe-Yosemite Trail is highly accessible. The backpacker who hates to confine his outings to one long vacation each summer can "do" most of the trail in a series of long weekends. The beginning knapsacker, just getting to know the wilderness, can sample portions of the trail on simple overnight trips or even day walks. The very ambitious walker can connect with the Muir Trail at Tuolumne Meadows and keep on walking to Mt. Whitney.

In this time of man's grave ecological crisis, when his future on earth is touch and go, a person needs to flee the city, leaving all the works of man behind, in order to renew his perspective on what matters, what counts. To fill that need, there are few better ways than to watch the sun set over a hidden lake in a purple, rocky bowl along the Tahoe-Yosemite Trail.

Gabbot Meadow cabin

HISTORY

The history of the Tahoe-Yosemite Trail will probably never be told. No one knows where all the documents are.

We checked the libraries; we talked or corresponded with everybody we could find who might know something of the trail's history. We found precious little information. For example, there were only two signs along the whole trail that said *Tahoe-Yosemite Trail*. They were both in the Eldorado National Forest, yet the Eldorado Supervisor didn't know when his jurisdiction had put them up. We are reasonably sure it was between 1917 and 1967, but not at all sure exactly when. A federal publication, *Trails for America* (1966), says the Tahoe-Yosemite Trail is one of seven sections of the Pacific Crest Trail, a continuous route from Canada to Mexico adopted by Congress in 1969. Yet the official Forest Service maps show that from Carson Pass to Grace Meadow in Yosemite–half of the entire Tahoe-Yosemite Trail–the two routes are separate.

Most Sierra buffs can tell you it was Theodore S. Solomons who conceived the idea of the John Muir Trail, but the parentage of the Tahoe-Yosemite Trail will remain moot. The first mention we can find of the trail is in the *Sierra Club Bulletin* of January 1917, which quotes from a memorandum by Coert Du Bois, head of the Forest Service in the California District:

> The Tahoe-Yosemite Trail . . . is proposed to afford an easy and attractive route from the Lake Tahoe region to the boundary of Yosemite National Park. Probably before it is completed the National Park authorities can be induced to complete the link between the head of Jack Main Canon and Tuolumne Meadows, which when done will connect the Tahoe-Yosemite Trail with the John Muir Trail. . . .
>
> I have a strong idea that such trails as the Tahoe-Yosemite Trail and John Muir Trail are going to be very popular in the future. Already every possible

> camping and recreation ground that can be reached with a Ford is getting overcrowded. The tendency is to get away from the crowd and take either a knapsack trip or a pack trip into the high country.
>
> During the field season of 1916 . . . the trail was completed up Meeks Creek past the Talent Lakes to Velma Lakes. . . . The trail is completed from Susie Lake to Desolation Valley with the exception of a very short stretch, and even this is passable for horses.
>
> On the Stanislaus section . . . the trail was completed from the head of Disaster Cañon to the east end of Iceberg, approximately six miles.

The next annual *Sierra Club Bulletin* (Jan. 1918) noted that

> During the 1917 field season the Forest Service completed the Tahoe-Yosemite Trail from Upper Echo Lake to the lower end of Echo Lake . . . The work was done in cooperation with the Western States Gas and Electric Co., which furnished most of the labor.

The third mention (and last, up to this writing) of the Tahoe-Yosemite Trail is a *Sierra Club Bulletin* appearing one year later, 1919, when the bulletin stated that the completion of the Tahoe-Yosemite Trail had been postponed because the U.S. was involved in World War I.

Meanwhile, in the summer of 1918, Vernon L. Bonner, Superintendent of Road Construction for the Forest Service in the area, traveled from Squaw Valley to the Yosemite border, in order to review a route for the Tahoe-Yosemite Trail which had been proposed within the Service; Bonner recommended some changes, mainly to cut construction costs. His recommended route to the Park border was 100 miles long, and he said, in 1918, that it would cost $38,200 to build the trail. In the fiscal years 1966-68, on the portion of the trail within the Eldorado National Forest alone, the Forest Service spent $189,000, much of it merely for maintenance.

Sometime around 1930, Clinton C. Clarke of Pasadena, California, began to promote what he called the Pacific Crest

Trailway. In 1932 he proposed the trail to the Forest Service and the Park Service. Evidently they adopted his proposal, for Clarke says that "at the end of the sixth year (1937) the Trail was a passable, continuous pathway from Canada to Mexico." Clarke's crusade for the trail was a one-man show. Clarke compiled his ideas in a book, *The Pacific Crest Trailway*, published in 1945. He described a route from Canada to Mexico roughly along the Cascade-Sierra backbone. Clarke divided the entire route into seven sections, one of which was the Tahoe-Yosemite Trail. In his book, the Tahoe-Yosemite Trail begins in the north at Yuba Pass, on State Route 49, and ends at Tuolumne Meadows, in the Yosemite high country. From Lake Tahoe's Meeks Bay, where the trail described in this book begins, Clarke's route follows our route except between Carson Pass and Kennedy Meadow.

And that, more or less, is how matters lay for 20 years. Then, in 1966, John Jencks of Berkeley, for 40 years a Sierra backpacker, started to write letters about the trail to the Forest Service. He asked them to send him a map showing the whole trail, if it existed. After many letters and one year's time, he finally received a map with a route traced on it. Jencks showed the map to us; then an erring packer performing as mail carrier lost the map somewhere south of Sequoia. We wrote the Forest Service for another tracing. The one they sent us differed from the previous one for the entire distance between Lake Alpine and Saucer Meadow, in the Stanislaus National Forest. Clearly, there was some question about the route.

We pored over our maps and tentatively picked out a route that we preferred; then we showed it to Harry Grace, Supervisor of the Stanislaus. He agreed with our judgment, and we began the happy task of walking the whole route to verify our map calculations.

As for the part of the trail in Yosemite National Park, there is just one obvious way to get from Bond Pass to Toulumne Meadows, and the Park Service informally regards that route as part of the Tahoe-Yosemite Trail.

Benwood Meadow—a fine flower garden

NATURAL HISTORY

Although most of the territory along the Tahoe-Yosemite Trail belongs legally to the United States Government, it belongs by right of possession to the plants and animals that live there, and that suffer us to make little visits. Some backpackers are nearly oblivious of all the organisms except perhaps the trees, but fortunately the ecology goes on without any attention from them. Other backpackers enter actively into this montane ecology, contemplating and conserving.

In this chapter we will offer a biased (our bias) sample of plants and animals and some generalities about the natural world along the Tahoe-Yosemite Trail. (For complete guides to the flora and fauna, see the bibliography at the end of this book.)

Every species fills its ecological *niche.* A niche is a way of life—the sum total of the organism's responses to temperature, wind, moisture, snow, soil, humidity, food, sunlight, disease, predators—and humans. No two species occupy the same niche, but some niches may overlap considerably. A number of species—a community—occupy a *habitat*, which is a place. Here, they coexist in a balanced way. For example, in a mountain meadow gophers fill the subterranean mammalian herbivore niche, and moles the subterranean mammalian carnivore niche.

Even if we don't know much about basic ecology, we can't help noticing that the natural scene along the Tahoe-Yosemite Trail changes dramatically with elevation. The most obvious changes are in the trees, just because trees are the most obvious—the largest—organisms. Furthermore, they don't move around, hide, or migrate in their lifetime, as do animals. When we pay close attention, we notice that not only the trees but the shrubs, flowers and grasses also change with elevation. Then we begin to find altitude differences in the animal populations. In other words, there are different *life zones*. A concept of life zones, still in use today, was formulated by C. Hart Merriam in 1898. Merriam divided North America into seven life zones, from the *Tropical* zone at the tip of Florida to the *Arctic* zone along the shores of the Arctic Ocean. Six of the seven zones occur in California. He also noted that if we ascend a high enough mountain, we pass through all the same zones that we would if we walked from Florida to the North Pole. It turns out that 100 feet of elevation are about equivalent to 17 miles of latitude. This means that, in terms of the living organisms, walking south from Meeks Bay to Tuolumne Meadows is like descending almost 500 feet. Therefore, if you could start out 500 feet *above* timberline near Meeks Bay and could walk on the level to the Tuolumne Meadows area, you would then be *at* timberline.

We can also correlate change in elevation with change in time of year, using the ratio of one day = 100 feet. If the mosquitoes hatch on June 23 at Susie Lake on the Tahoe-Yosemite Trail, they should hatch on June 24 at Heather Lake, which is 100 feet higher. Obviously, a careful planner could spend his whole summer in a cloud of mosquitoes. More felicitously, he could watch flowers of the same species bloom every day–until he got beyond their habitats.

The table of life zones below gives some typical plants and animals for each of the six life zones found in California. The last four are found along the Tahoe-Yosemite Trail. As the table shows, the elevation ranges overlap. There are several reasons why. Besides the differences in latitude, the elevational life-zone boundaries depend on differences in such things as slope (north- or south-facing) and moisture.

As we walk the Tahoe-Yosemite Trail we can learn to tell what life zone we are in, we can identify many different habitats, and we can conceptualize the niches in them by observing what the different animals we see "do for a living." The natural history "notes" below describe only a small sampling of some plants and animals that inhabit Tahoe-Yosemite Trail country, but they may start you looking into things for yourself. (We have given the scientific names with the common names because common names vary in different books.)

ZONE	ELEVATION	TYPICAL PLANTS AND ANIMALS
Lower Sonoran	less than 500	Valley oak, mesquite, bell vireo, yellow warbler, yellow-billed magpie, cottontail rabbit, kit fox.
Upper Sonoran	500 to 3-4000	buckbrush, blue oak, digger pine, chaparral mouse, California jay, gray fox.
Transition	3-4000 to 6-7000	Ponderosa pine, sugar pine, incense cedar, Douglas fir, mountain misery, mountain dogwood, pygmy nuthatch, spotted owl, gray squirrel.
Canadian	6-7000 to 8-9000	Jeffrey pine, silver pine, red fir, huckleberry oak, bush chinquapin, mountain pocket gopher, Hammond flycatcher, sooty lodgepole chipmunk, grouse, Williamson's sapsucker.
Hudsonian	8-9000 to 11,000	Mountain hemlock, whitebark pine, red heather, white heather, pine grosbeak, Clark nutcracker, belding ground squirrel, cony.
Arctic-Alpine	above 11,000	(no trees), alpine willow, rosy finch.

BIRDS

Golden eagle *(Aquila chrysaetos)* The golden eagle is in essence a hawk of majestic proportions. The largest bird in the region, it is a resident throughout the Sierra. It commonly breeds in the Upper Sonoran and Transition zones, but may be seen above timberline in the summer. Its length is about 3 feet, its wingspread about 7 feet. From a distance the bird looks almost uniformly dark-colored, but at close range we can see light golden brown on the head, neck and upper back. The female is the larger sex. The golden eagle feeds mainly on squirrels and rabbits, and like other squirrel hawks, it does not have the ferocity that some people ascribe to it.

Sooty grouse *(Dendragapus fuliginosus)* Also called the dusky or the blue grouse, this large bird waddles conspicuously when it walks, whirrs when it flies, and ventriloquizes when it talks. Finding a perch in a crotch of a red fir, the male emits a note that almost defies localizing by human ears, and it defies spelling too, sounding something like "boont" or "wunt." The bird is 16-19 inches long, generally dark gray, with relatively short wings and a blackish tail with a whitish band at its end. It eats mainly the tips of pine and fir needles, and nests on the ground.

Oregon junco *(Junco oreganus)* This very common summer visitor to the highlands frequents a wide variety of habitats, especially meadows and fairly moist woodlands. The head and neck are black or grayish black, the body mostly brownish, and the tail blackish except for white outer tail-feathers. These white feathers are very noticeable in flight, and along with the habit of traveling in flocks, are almost enough for sure identification. The junco is a ground forager, hopping about in willowy meadows to discover weed seeds and insects. It nests on the ground and occasionally in trees. Along the Tahoe-Yosemite Trail you will probably see more juncoes than any other bird.

Water ouzel *(Cinclus mexicanus)* This songbird, related to thrushes and wrens, has adopted wading and diving habits, probably because there wasn't any "normal" aquatic bird occupying such a niche. We find the ouzel around falls and fast water along streams in the Transition, Canadian and Hudsonian zones. It not only dives but actually walks along the bottom of a rushing stream, feeding on aquatic insects, like caddis flies, water bugs and beetles. The ouzel's adaptations to water include an oil gland on its tail that is about 10 times as large as the gland in its terrestrial cousins, from which it spreads oil to all its feathers as it preens. It also has a movable, scaly cover over each nostril which closes when it is underwater. When the bird alights on a rock, it bobs up and down, and this behavior has led some people to call it by the friendly name of "dipper." The bird nests in a ball of moss about one foot in diameter, beside a stream, usually at the base of a cliff or between several rocks. Given its habits, you

Crag Lake

should be able to identify it without any physical description, but the description is simple: chunky, slate-gray, short-tailed and smaller than a robin.

WILDFLOWERS

Lupine *(Lupinus breweri)* You can't spend much time out of doors in California without learning about lupine, and this genus of the pea family is well-represented in the High Sierra. The genus is named from the Latin *lupus*, wolf, based on the idea that lupines rob the soil. Actually, being legumes, they replenish it with nitrogen. The species we describe (like many other High Sierra species of plants and animals) is named for William Brewer, who led the marvelously successful geological survey parties in the Sierra in 1863 and 1864. The flower is blue, with the typical pea-family flower shape: a "banner" of two petals, 2 "wings" of one petal each, and a "keel" of one petal. A lupine plant is low and matted, with compound leaves of 7-10 leaflets arranged in a rosette around the stem attachment. Lupine probably forms the largest fields of any flower along the Tahoe-Yosemite Trail. A blue field of it, sometimes understoried by grass and sometimes growing in bare decomposed granite, may be several hundred yards long.

Shooting star *(Dodecatheon jeffreyi)* Whenever we come to a wet meadow, we can expect to see hundreds or thousands of these asymmetrical flowers with lavender or magenta petals that curve back closely upon the flower stem. The name of the genus means "the 12 gods," but it is not clear why. The species is named for John Jeffreys, as is one species of Sierra pine. Jeffreys was a botanist who tromped the west looking for new species, found several and one day disappeared in the desert. Shooting star has a large altitudinal range, from Upper Sonoran to Arctic-Alpine.

Mountain pennyroyal *(Monardella odoratissima)* The species name of this flower means that it stinks a lot, and it does, but the smell is to most hikers a pleasant one. On sunny slopes in the early afternoon of warm days, the fragrance makes us stop, savor it, and look around for the source. Pennyroyal is a mint, and it can be brewed into a passable tea.

The plant has many small pale purple flowers in a dense head, and like other mints it has leaves in opposed pairs along the stem.

Penstemon *(Penstemon spp.)* ("spp." is botanical shorthand for "one or another species.") Along the Tahoe-Yosemite Trail we encounter four main penstemons and several rarer ones. The common ones are mountain pride *(P. newberryi)*, Bridges' penstemon *(P. Bridgesii)*, whorled penstemon *(P. heterodoxus)* and Davidson's penstemon *(P. Davidsonii)*.

The penstemons are as widespread as any genus along the Tahoe-Yosemite Trail. Sometimes we see only one in a mile, but sometimes we find them filling a series of long cracks in a granite ledge, and sometimes in a lake we see an island whose gray granite is nearly hidden by the red or scarlet blossoms of penstemon. The tubular flower has an upper lip with two lobes and a lower lip with three. The genus gets its name from the five stamens ("pent" = five in Latin) which all penstemons have. A stamen, a male reproductive organ, consists of a long, thin filament tipped by a small, compact anther. In this genus, one stamen is sterile, and it usually is bearded–hence the alternative name of penstemons, "beard tongue." Above 10,000 feet you will probably encounter only two species, and you can probably be sure of your identification: *heterodoxus* if the flowers come out from the stem in a ring, or whorl, and *Davidsonii* if they don't.

Indian Paintbrush *(Castilleja spp.)* The showy color of paintbrush is due not to its flower, which is small, but to structures called bracts, which we can think of as being intermediate between petals and leaves. (The poinsettia of lower elevations, for instance, has even more showy bracts.) The flower itself is small and usually greenish. There are at least half a dozen species in the high country, some of which flourish down to 2000 feet elevation. Most species inhabit wet areas, but the small, not-very-reddish species called *nana* prefers dry, rocky places. One paintbrush or another will be in bloom almost any time that we are likely to be walking the trail.

TREES

Sugar pine *(Pinus lambertiana)* This is the largest of all the pines, and it was John Muir's favorite Sierra tree. We don't see many sugar pines along the Tahoe-Yosemite Trail, because they they grow only up to about 7000 feet elevation. One of the highest stands is on the Fallen Leaf lateral approach to the Tahoe-Yosemite Trail, around Glen Alpine Spring. We also see it around Kennedy Meadow and in the Mokelumne River canyon.

The name "sugar" comes from the white, sugarlike substance that forms in drops on the bark or wood when the heartwood is wounded. Botanically, sugar is one of the white pines, which are distinguished by having five needles in a bundle. Thus it is a cousin of higher-dwelling western white pine, which overlaps its range in the Canadian zone.

The sugar pine, which has a life span of about 500 years, is the largest organism on the Tahoe-Yosemite Trail. Trees 160-180 feet tall and 4-7 feet in diameter are common, and heights of 245 feet and diameters of 18 feet have been reported.

The blue-green needles are 2½-4 inches long; the reddish-brown bark is 2-3 inches thick, and deeply grooved. But perhaps the oustanding feature of *lambertiana* is its cones. Largest of all pine cones, they reach a length of 20 inches or more and a diameter of 6 inches. Hanging from the tips of long, graceful branches, they epitomize the reproductive power of the plant kingdom.

Whitebark pine *(Pinus albicaulis)* Our approach to timberline along the Tahoe-Yosemite Trail is heralded by lonely, bushy, stunted pine trees. Exposed to extreme changes of temperature, fierce winds and long periods of snow, the whitebark pine occurs occasionally in scattered stands, more often as isolated individuals. A little below timberline, as between Carson Pass and Winnemucca Lake, the tree is erect if not very tall (15-30 feet), but at slightly higher elevations the tree is prostrate, and at timberline its gnarled and twisted multiple trunks wind among the rocks, as if it were a lost traveler seeking protection from the elements.

If life at timberline is tough, it doesn't prevent longevity in *albicaulis*. In *The Mountains of California* John Muir wrote that he counted 255 annual rings in a tree less than 3 feet high, and other whitebarks have been found over 400 years old.

Whitebark needles make bundles of five, dark green in color and 1½-2½ inches long. They form clusters near the tips of branchlets. The young cones are a striking purple color, 1-3 inches long. They turn yellow-brown by the end of the second summer, and unlike the cones of any other North American pine they disintegrate on the tree and fall to the ground, scale by scale.

Ponderosa pine *(Pinus ponderosa)* Whereas the sugar pine is largely confined to California, ponderosa grows in all the western states. There is more standing wood in ponderosa trees than in any other pine in North America.

Some people call it yellow pine, after the light yellowish-tan color of the bark of mature trees. This color plus the long yellow-green needles (5-10 inches) will identify the tree for you from a distance, once you have practiced making the identification. At first, you may confuse ponderosa with another pine which some botanists say is merely a variety of it, and some say is a separate species—Jeffrey pine. The confusion is ended by making the nose test: place your nose in a furrow between bark plates, and inhale. If you detect a smell that reminds you of either vanilla or pineapple, you have a Jeffrey. The cone-tossing test will confirm the diagnosis: toss a cone and catch it. If the prickles on the ends of the scales stick your hand, you have a ponderosa; otherwise, you were right—it's a Jeffrey.

Ponderosa grows in pure stands and in mixtures with other trees in a wide variety of soils, sites and elevations. Although it shows a preference for sunny climates and warm situations, it is able to endure severe winters. Having a deep taproot and long, strong side roots, the tree can resist drought well. Ponderosa forests are nearly always rather open, because the tree does not like shade, and because the far-reaching roots are competing for moisture. Not as large as a sugar pine, the ponderosa is still up to 230 feet tall and 8 feet thick.

Lodgepole pines *National Park Service*

Lodgepole pine *(Pinus murrayana)* This conifer is the commonest tree along the Tahoe-Yosemite Trail. It grows over a wide range of elevations, from as low as 6300 feet along Meeks Creek, to as high as 10,000 feet in the vicinity of Bond Pass. There are even a few lodgepoles at 4000 feet in Yosemite Valley.

Identification is easy, because lodgepoles are the only two-needle pines along the Tahoe-Yosemite Trail. Lodgepole bark is also unlike the bark of other pines, being much thinner and having much smaller scales.

Because lodgepoles tolerate wet soil they have been given the unkind epithet of "meadow murderers." They are the first trees to invade a meadow, after stream deposition has turned a glacially created lake into a meadow. Photographs taken 50 years ago of various high meadows show far fewer lodgepoles than do recent photographs. The Indians used to set periodic fires in the Sierra to keep the meadows open.

A common sight in the high country is a lodgepole snag, a tree that has died and lost its bark and its branches, but still stands, straight and sun-burnished. We notice that a spiral grain is very evident in the dead trunk, and then we notice that it always spirals the same way. Some backpackers attribute the spiral to an owl that sits on top and from time to time rotates a little without letting go. They are wrong. Spiral growth is nearly universal in trees, and it is genetically determined. Evolution has selected for it because it gives greater strength than straight growth would. Environment works within the limits of heredity to determine the degree of spiraling. Since spirals are for strength, we find that trees which grow in windier places spiral more.

What is perhaps more surprising is that the spiral changes direction as you cut into the tree. Thus a spiral that is right-handed on the outside may be left-handed on the inside. The tightness of the coils—that is, the slope of the grain—may also change.

Mountain hemlock *(Tsuga mertensiana)* If Muir preferred the sugar among all the pines, he reserved his highest accolade for one of the highest-dwelling conifers along the Tahoe-

Yosemite Trail: mountain hemlock. It is hard to disagree with him. The hemlock's lightness of form contrasts with the more rugged trees around it; its dark green older foliage is set off by its pale blue-green new growth; and its leaning leader, or tip, is the epitome of grace. Yet, as Muir said, the best words only hint at its claims; come to the mountains and see.

The short needles of hemlock thickly clothe the lateral branchlets, being attached all around the twig. The cones, 2 inches long and bluish-purple in color, are borne throughout the upper part of the tree. In the lower parts of its elevation range, the hemlock grows to 100 feet in height, and develops a trunk several feet thick that is branch-free up to 30 feet or so. But near timberline, the tree may have a sprawling bush shape.

Hemlock wood is especially flexible, and the young trees are bent to the ground by snow every winter. A novice hiker is often startled by the whiplike sound of a hemlock when its snow load has melted enough to allow the tree's own elastic energy to suddenly snap it upright, throwing a shower of snow from its branches.

Sierra juniper *(Juniperus occidentalis)* No one has yet been able to write about this tree without using the word "gnarled," though some authors have managed to eschew "picturesque." The Sierra (or western) juniper is a member of the cypress family, and so a cousin of the pines and firs within the order of conifers. We recognize it by its highly asymmetrical shape, its cypresslike leaves—tiny, overlapping, scalelike leaves closely pressed to the twigs—its cinnamon-brown, shreddy bark, and its small round berries.

The juniper usually grows on a desolate, windswept slope, far from any other tree. Long, exposed roots cling to small cracks at the base of the stocky, buttressed trunk. The juniper does not grow tall—perhaps up to 30 feet—because it is continually being dismembered by snow avalanches, lightning and high winds. On the side most exposed to storms, branches may be dead or missing; on the other side, they may stand out almost horizontally. Both the pattern of foliage and the arrangement of branches are highly irregular.

Aspen *(Populus tremuloides)* Since most high-country trees are evergreens, fall foliage is not as colorful as in the eastern U.S. But in September and October, the quaking aspen tree, along with various willows, provides color enough. The somber, green-clad mountainsides of the upper elevations are dotted with brilliant patches of bright golden yellow and orange as the aspen prepare to drop their year's leaves.

Aspen is the most conspicuous broadleaved tree in the Canadian and Hudsonian zones. It can easily be identified by its smooth, white bark and its fluttering leaves, whose thin flat stems allow them to tremble in the slightest breeze. On older trees, the bark turns rough and dark at the base of the trunk, and this change progresses up the trunk with age.

Like all poplars, aspens prefer moist, sandy soils, and we find them usually along streams. A grove of aspen in an alluvial flat covered by springtime grasses is no less handsome than the same grove in its autumn showiness. The appearance of a few aspen on a rocky hillside betrays the presence of a spring.

Unlike a conifer, which bears cones of both sexes, an aspen tree is either male or female. The male tree produces tassels with deep red stamens; the female produces cottony tassels with seeds.

MAMMALS

Sierra chickaree *(Tamiasciurus douglasii)* This little squirrel disturbs your peace when you disturb his. Walking quietly along a duff trail under the trees, you will suddenly hear a loud, accusing "kwir-o" followed by a series of squeals and squeaks that sound like remonstration if not rodential profanity. Somewhere in the conifer tops is a chickaree, sentry for the whole forest.

The chickaree, also called the red squirrel, is about one third the size of the more familiar gray squirrel, with a much less bushy tail. The back is red-tinged, the underside is whitish, and a black stripe down the side divides the two areas. This squirrel lives in the Transition, Canadian and Hudsonian zones, usually making its home in a tree cavity which it has lined with hair and various plant materials. Its main source of food is cone seeds, and not being a hibernator, it harvests a supply of cones for the winter. The chickaree cuts off a number of fir or pine cones, then rushes down the tree trunk to drag them to a cache near home. He can work very fast: the record we have read about is 13 cones cut in 10 seconds! Somewhere along the Tahoe-Yosemite Trail you might find yourself in a sudden squall of pine cones.

Since the squirrel eats the seeds only, it soon creates quite a pile of scales and stems. You can find these "kitchen middens" throughout the forested high country.

Golden-mantled ground squirrel *(Citellus lateralis)* The head, neck and shoulders of this beautiful ground squirrel are a reddish or copper-toned yellow, and they form the "golden mantle." A broad white stripe runs along each side of the blue-gray back, between two dark stripes. These stripes lead some people to confuse the animal with a chipmunk, but the golden-mantle is larger than any chipmunk (about 11 inches overall) and does not have stripes running across its face. Golden-mantles are common in the open forests of the Canadian and Hudsonian zones. They make short burrows underground, with the entrance near a log, stump or rock which provides a lookout point.

This rodent eats a wide variety of plant food—seeds, blossoms, leaves, berries, mushrooms, roots, bulbs and pine nuts—and meat, including insects, when it can get any. It also will steal a cone felled by a chickaree before the little harvester can get down to cache the cone.

Yellow-bellied marmot *(Marmota flaviventris)* Chances are better than even that a marmot is the largest animal you will see on any given backpack in the Sierra. This chunky member of the ground-squirrel tribe, sometimes as much as 2 feet long, is easy to identify. He inhabits rocky terrain, and talus slopes are his special favorite, for he likes to spend a large part of the day sunning himself on a rock. If you don't pass too close, he will not rise from his sun bath, and you can get a good look at his coat. The upper parts are grizzled yellowish brown; the underparts are dull orange-yellow. The dark bushy tail is about 7 inches long. The marmot has a whitish patch around his eyes, and a dark band over his nose.

When alarmed, the marmot sounds a shrill whistle and rushes for his burrow under a rock. But if you wait a little while, he'll poke out his head for another look. This fat fellow feeds mainly on grass and leafy green plants, stoking up in the short summer for a hibernation that may last as long as nine months. We may see marmots in the Canadian, Hudsonian and Arctic-Alpine zones.

FISH

Brook trout *(Salvelinus fontinalis)* One of the commonest animals along the Tahoe-Yosemite Trail is not even a native. The brook trout has been introduced into high lakes and streams by the state Department of Fish and Game. Native to the eastern U.S., as far west as Iowa, the "brookie" has been successfully introduced into all the western mountain areas.

To the novice, trout look pretty much alike, but it takes only a little practice to become able to distinguish a brook trout, even when it is in the water. In the water, we can see the whiteness of the front edge of the pectoral fins. Seen out of the water, the back, dorsal fin and tail are mostly dark olive green, but light, wavy lines interrupt the dark area. The light spots on the sides are cream-colored or red, the red spots often encircled in blue. The lower fins are reddish-orange. In spawning season (fall) the male's underside becomes a brilliant red or orange. Altogether the fish is extremely handsome.

The reason for the widespread planting of the brook trout in Sierra lakes is that he likes cold water and he can spawn in still water. He can perpetuate his kind even though the inlet and outlet of a lake have gone virtually dry. Rainbow, brown and golden trout almost have to have moving water.

Brook trout are easier to catch than the others. A brookie will take bait, spoons and other lures, wet flies and dry flies—striking more than once at the fly if it misses the first time. The pink meat of *Salvelinus* is rated by many anglers as the finest of any trout meat.

GEOLOGY

California is a land of superlatives. It has the highest point in the contiguous United States, and the lowest. It has the tallest living thing, and the oldest. Indeed, when scientists finally discovered that the giant sequoia of California was not the oldest living thing after all, where in the world did the *new* oldest living thing–the bristlecone pine–turn out to live? In California!

In the realm of geology, California has the longest and largest continuous mountain range in the United States–the Sierra Nevada. The Cascades, the Appalachians and the Rockies are all longer, but each is a series of ranges, not a single range. The Sierra is a single uplifted and tilted section of the earth's crust, 430 miles long and 40-80 miles wide. This block of the earth's crust is large enough to bear on its back peaks and ridges that loom above the hiker like Brobdignagian battlements; yet these peaks and ridges are no more than corrugations on the surface of the great Sierra block.

What created this great block range?

Almost every part of the earth's crust has been below sea level many times since the seas were formed. Each time, sediments piled up on the sinking sea bottom to a depth of as much as 10 or 20 miles. Later, the accumulated sediment, turned to rock, rose above the sea, being heaved up and buckled by titanic earth forces that are still only dimly understood. Then the new land was eroded by water, wind, and–sometimes–ice. These earth processes were repeated again and again in the area we call the Sierra.

During one of the periods of elevation, about 130 million years ago, an inconceivably large amount of molten granite welled up from deep within the crust and invaded the overlying strata, melting its way upward into the older rocks. But it never reached the surface; it cooled and solidified at a depth of miles.

Since then erosion has removed ancient sediments 9-17 miles thick from above this granite, exposing it over most of the range. In fact, many people think of the Sierra as being all granite, though as we shall see it is not.

Finally, just a few million years ago, the upthrusting forces asserted themselves very strongly, and they raised the Sierra to roughly its present height. The land to the east rose right along along with what is now the Sierra, and the result was a broad arch that extended many miles beyond the present crest (see the figure below). A mere 750,000 years ago or less, the range began to take on the form we see today, with its steep eastern slope. Earth forces of unimaginable power created a series of faults in the vicinity of the eastern edge of the present range, and pieces of the crust on the east side of this fault system dropped down thousands of feet (at the rate of a few inches a year), while the Sierra block stayed high. Other faults developed farther east, and vertical movements along them created other valleys, between other ranges, such as Death Valley.

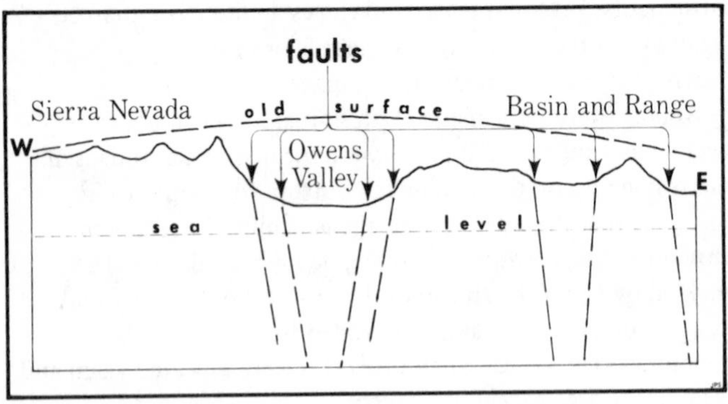

Lake Tahoe was formed during this recent period of great deformation. The Tahoe basin was created when a block of crust in the Sierra sank between two faults that separate the basin from the Carson Range on the east and from the Mt. Tallac-Squaw Peak range on the west. The bottom of Lake Tahoe, which is the floor of the Tahoe basin, is as low as the floor of the Carson Valley in western Nevada, so that the lake is very deep—about 1600 feet deep.

By a geological coincidence, the uplifting of the Sierra to its present elevation coincided with changes in the earth's climate which led to an ice age. After the great upthrust, the Sierra was high enough (and hence cold enough) for ice to exist the year around. Less than a million years ago, ice fields formed around the summits of the range, grew, and merged until they covered an area about 270 miles long and 20-30 miles wide, except for the higher peaks and divides. Even these were generally covered in the upper basins of the Tuolumne and Stanislaus rivers. Glaciers flowed—for obviously ice does flow—far down the river canyons to the west. The Tuolumne glacier extended as far west as Hetch Hetchy, 60 miles from its fountains among the highest peaks, and it was 4000 feet thick in the Grand Canyon of the Tuolumne River. (This canyon, so named, is in fact as deep as the Grand Canyon in Arizona, a mile deep.)

This ice sculptured the landscape we see today as we walk the Tahoe-Yosemite Trail. The glaciers simply took the rock from one place and put it in another. The power they had was great enough to make big canyons out of little ones, tear down mountain peaks, and scoop out lake basins hundreds of feet deep. The steep peaks and divides that characterize the Sierra are the result of glaciers "eating" headward at the upper ends of their valleys. Children at the beach sometimes play a game in which each child in turn, using the edge of his hand, scoops away some sand from near a match sticking out of the sand. The loser of the game is the child who took the last scoop before the match toppled. Ice action at the upper end of a glacier does the same thing as the child's hand. Above the ice surface, *frost-wedging* pries chunks of rock out of the steep mountainside by alternately freezing and thawing the water that seeps into tiny cracks in the rock. The pried-out boulders tumble down onto the ice at the upper end of the glacier. Beneath the ice, at the bottom of the large crevass that develops at the head of every glacier, similar freezing and thawing loosens blocks of rock, and then the moving ice pulls them out and carries them away, This latter action is called *quarrying.*

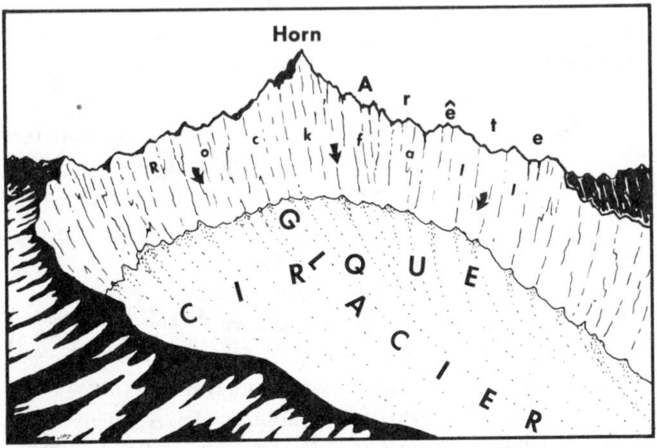

The amphitheaterlike bowl that a glacier creates in its upper reaches is called a *cirque*. Two examples along the Tahoe-Yosemite Trail are the bowls that contain Dicks Lake and Fourth of July Lake. Two cirques being eroded headward toward the divide that separates them eventually create a knifelike ridge called an *arête*; three or more create a spiry peak called a *horn*. Two examples of arêtes are the divide at Dicks Pass and the ridge east of Relief Peak. Matterhorn Peak, on the northeast border of Yosemite, is a horn.

By frost-wedging and quarrying, a glacier acquires a set of cutting and grinding tools–great rocks frozen into its bottom and sides–which it uses to abrade the canyon down which it flows. If the bedrock underneath is extensively jointed (laced with cracks), the glacial erosion will create a valley that is U-shaped in cross section, like Yosemite Valley. A combination of quarrying and abrasion beneath the ice deepens the canyon and cuts off the spurs of side canyons. If, on the other hand, the rock is what geologists call "massive," meaning unjointed, it will resist the attacks of the glaciers. It is not susceptible to the ice-cracking, lifting and plucking by which glaciers do their work. This accounts for valleys that remained V-shaped, like

Summit City canyon. In such places glacial erosion was restricted primarily to rasping and polishing because of the massive, unjointed rock facade presented to the ice—it simply couldn't get a "bite."

At the lower end of the glacier, supply and demand are equal: the rate at which flowing ice arrives there just balances the rate of melting, and, as the economists would tell us, there is equilibrium. As the terminal ice melts, it drops its load of rock, gravel, sand and silt, which form a terminal moraine. The glacier has already dropped some of its load along its side margins, forming lateral moraines. And when the climate warms and the glacier recedes back into the highlands, it drops the rest of its load in place, as ground moraine. The recession may temporarily stop several times; each time another terminal moraine, or recessional moraine, will form. Unlike sedimentary deposits in bodies of water, glacial deposits are not sorted according to particle size and are not laminated into beds. Many High Sierra lakes were created by terminal moraines acting as dams. Examples are Gilmore Lake and Fallen Leaf Lake.

In the Sierra there were at least four glacial stages, separated by periods during which the climate was warmer than it is today. The last stage reached its maximum about 55,000 years ago and ended only 9500 years ago. By that time, all the glaciers had melted. The ones we see today have been formed in the last 4000 years, due to a recent cooling of the climate. These present-day glaciers are younger than the Pyramid of Cheops!

Although the Sierra is a single piece of the earth's crust, its rocks vary widely in origin, in chemical composition, in color, in density, in structure and in age. The greatest geological variety in the entire range is found along the Tahoe-Yosemite Trail. Granite, gabbro, diorite, aplite, latite, andesite, slate, schist, monzonite, limestone, marble—these rocks and many more can be identified along this trail. Some, like the granite, were formed deep within the crust by slow cooling of molten rock. Some were formed by quick cooling of volcanic flows and volcanic explosions at the surface. Some were formed by compaction of layers of silt and sand that had been deposited in ancient seas. And some were formed from pre-existing rocks by the action of intense heat and pressure.

During the great deformation of the last 10 million years—and even a little earlier—an immense amount of volcanic activity took place in the Sierra north of Yosemite. Unlike the molten granite, the mineral soup of this period found its way to the surface, by rising up the faults in the crust. Some of the lava was quietly extruded, like the Hawaiian flows of today, and some of it was blown out in violent explosions, like the explosion of Krakatau. This liquid rock flowed down the valleys—or floated, if airborne—came to rest, and solidified. Eventually the deposits were thick enough to cover all the northern Sierra except a few high peaks like Pyramid Peak. The eroded remnants of these volcanic rocks, interspersed with the famous granite, are what give the Tahoe-Yosemite Trail its great variety of rocks and of landforms. The volcanic rocks are of so many colors—deep umber, gray, brown, rust, black, ochre, sienna, green—depending on their original minerals and on how much they have been oxidized since they were formed. The fact that the lava and ash were deposited in layers, unlike the granite, is responsible for the stepped sets of cliffs we see in much of the northern Sierra: on Stevens Peak, Dardanelles Cone, Leavitt Peak, Relief Peak, and many others. Some layers are hard and some are soft—as rocks go—and the hard layers of course make the cliffs.

Even the granite has a great variety. A geological study of the Fallen Leaf Lake quadrangle describes ten different kinds of granite in the Desolation Valley area. Some granite is very light-colored, almost white—one reason Muir called the Sierra Nevada the "Range of Light"—and some is quite dark, due to a high content of alkaline minerals, named biotite and hornblende.

One of the distinctive bodies of granite is the Cathedral Peak granite, which we come to at about the 8100-foot level beside the Tuolumne River (if walking up the canyon). This rock is characterized by large crystals (up to 6") of darker potassium feldspar set in a groundmass of microscopic, lighter-colored crystals of quartz and plagioclase feldspar. The large crystals resist erosion better than the smaller ones, so on weathered Cathedral Peak granite they stand out as bumps on the main mass.

There is no better way to see all this geological wonder than to walk the Tahoe-Yosemite Trail. The hiker who wants to identify the rocks along the way should take a manual and a magnifying glass, and perhaps one of the detailed rock maps available from the State Division of Mines and Geology. Others will simply look and contemplate the last few hundred million years.

The Dardanelles

Trailhead Map

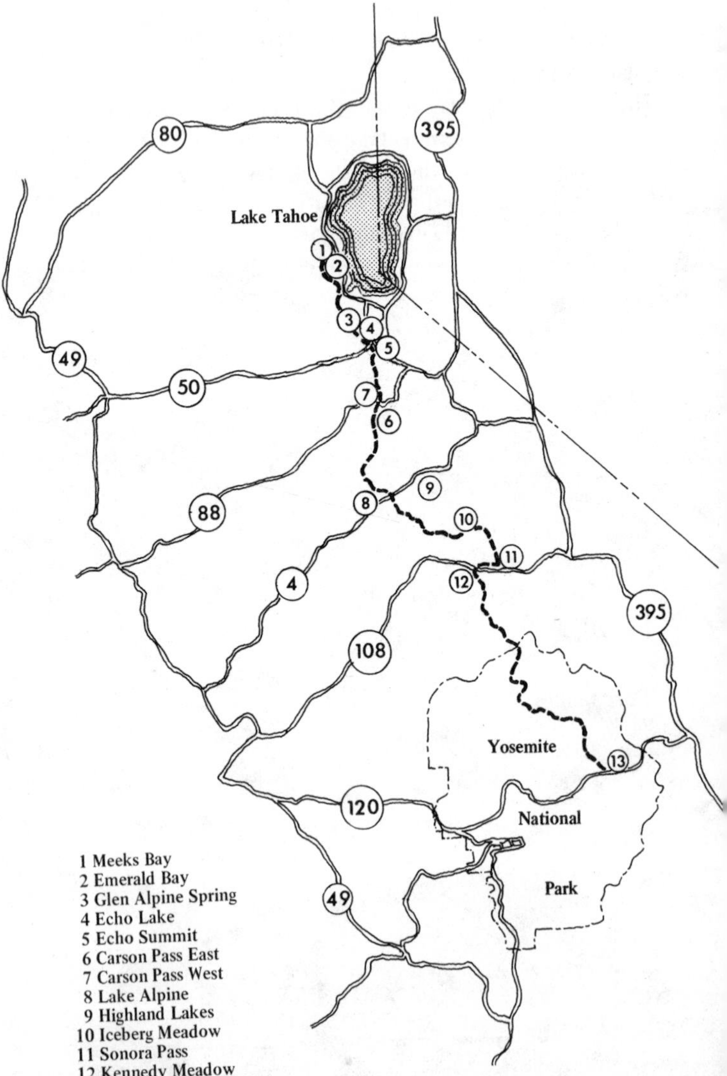
80
395
Lake Tahoe
1
2
3
4
5
49
50
7
6
9
8
88
10
11
12
4
395
108
Yosemite
13
120
National
Park
49
1 Meeks Bay
2 Emerald Bay
3 Glen Alpine Spring
4 Echo Lake
5 Echo Summit
6 Carson Pass East
7 Carson Pass West
8 Lake Alpine
9 Highland Lakes
10 Iceberg Meadow
11 Sonora Pass
12 Kennedy Meadow
13 Tuolumne Meadows

TRAILHEADS and CAMPGROUNDS

Throughout its length the Tahoe-Yosemite Trail has a variety of access points. Here is a list of the trailheads for the Tahoe-Yosemite Trail and the public campgrounds and resorts near them, listed from north to south. (The numbers refer to locations on the trailhead map.)

1. **Meeks Bay Trailhead.** Across from a parking area near Meeks Bay Resort on Highway 89 along the west shore of Lake Tahoe.

2. **Emerald Bay Trailheads.** At the west end of Emerald Bay, on Highway 89 along the west shore of Lake Tahoe. One trailhead is at Eagle Falls Picnic Ground, the other at Bayview Picnic Ground.

3. **Glen Alpine Spring Trailhead.** One mile up a dirt road from the head of Fallen Leaf Lake.

4. **Echo Lake Trailhead.** 1½ miles north of Highway 50 at the end of a road that leaves the highway just west of Echo Summit. The upper boat landing is 2 miles from there by boat-taxi, available at the Echo Resort docks.

5. **Echo Summit Trailhead.** At the end of a short ski-resort spur road that leads south from just west of Echo Summit.

6. **Carson Pass East Trailhead.** 0.1 mile east of Carson Pass down the old highway, at a sign in a little parking lot.

7. **Carson Pass West Trailhead.** 0.3 mile west of the pass in a parking lot.

8. **Lake Alpine Trailhead.** Fifty miles east of Angels Camp on Highway 4.

9. **Highland Lakes Trailhead.** Seven miles south of Highway 4, which you leave at a point 1.5 miles west of Ebbetts Pass. The trailhead is at the south end of Lower Highland Lake.

10. **Iceberg Meadow Trailhead.** At the end of a 9-mile blacktop highway that leaves the Sonora Pass Highway 20 miles east of the Pinecrest **Y**.

11. Sonora Pass Trailhead. One mile west of Sonora Pass on Highway 108.

12. Kennedy Meadow Trailhead. One mile up an oiled road from Highway 108, 29 miles east of the Pinecrest **Y**.

13. Tuolumne Meadows Trailhead. Thirty-nine miles east of Crane Flat on Highway 120, just beyond a bridge over the Tuolumne River.

CAMPGROUNDS

The human body is more efficient on the trail if it gets a chance to acclimate to high altitudes for a few hours before going to work. If you possibly can, sleep overnight somewhere near your trailhead on the Tahoe-Yosemite Trail. Below is a list of government campgrounds, arranged north-to-south, near the Tahoe-Yosemite Trail.

Campground	Elevation	Location
Fallen Leaf	6300 ft.	4 mi. from U.S. 50 via 89 plus side road
Woods Lake	8200	1 mi. S. of Highway 88, from 1 mi. E. of Caples Lake
Caples Lake	7800	On Highway 88, 63 mi. E. of Jackson
Silver Lake	7200	Beyond N. end of Silver Lake, 52 mi. E. of Jackson
Highland Lakes	8600	7 mi. W. of Highway 4, from 14 mi. E. of Lake Alpine
Lake Alpine	7400	W. end of Lake Alpine
Silver Valley	7400	E. end of Lake Alpine
Pine Marten	7400	E. end of Lake Alpine
Silvertip	7500	2/3 mi. W. of Lake Alpine
Campgrounds (2)	6200 ca.	Along dead end Clark Fork road off Highway 108
Campgrounds (7)	6200 ca.	Between Clark Fork turnoff and Kennedy Meadow turnoff on Highway 108

Chipmunk Flat	8400	73 mi. E. of Sonora on Highway 108
Tuolumne Meadows	8400	In Tuolumne Meadows on Highway 120

For last-minute purchases of provisions and for a place to leave your car (at your own risk) there are several resorts near the Tahoe-Yosemite Trail. They do not have food of backpacking quality or weight. Four of them have associated pack stations.

Name of Resort	Highway	Supplies	Parking	Pack Stock
Fallen Leaf	off 89	x	x	
Echo Lakes	off 50	x	x	
Caples Lake	88	x	x	
Kit Carson	88	x	x	
Kay's Silver Lake	88	x	x	
Lake Alpine	4	x	x	
Dardanelles	108	x	x	
Kennedy Meadow	108	x	fee	x
Tuolumne Meadows	120	x	x	x

Emergency services are available in the cities and towns of South Lake Tahoe, Jackson, Angels Camp, Sonora, Yosemite Valley and Lee Vining.

The
TRAIL

INTRODUCTION TO TRAIL DESCRIPTIONS

Terminology

Our description of the Tahoe-Yosemite Trail in the following chapters is an effort to describe what is along the trail, and the route to be followed. In general the trail is well signed (directions indicated by signs on signposts or trees). Where the signs are missing or unclear, we have attempted to give clear directions. (By the time you read this, the Forest Service and the Park Service may have put up more signs.) Sometimes the route is marked by ducks or cairns. A duck is one or several small rocks placed upon a larger rock or boulder in such a manner that the placement is obviously not natural. A cairn is a number of small rocks made into a pile. Sometimes the route is blazed (marked by tree blazes, where some bark has been slashed from tree trunks). In Yosemite, the blaze is usually a distinctive "T." The "T" blaze was first used when the U.S. cavalry administered the Park.

Grade

To indicate the amount of slope, up or down, we have used four terms. These terms, with their meanings, are:

level

gentle

moderate

steep

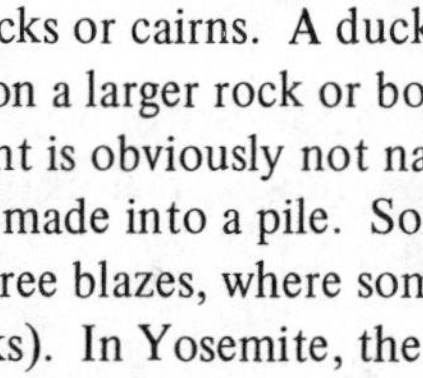

Forest density

To indicate the density of the forest cover (and hence, inversely, the exposure to the sun) we have used four terms:

barren

sparse 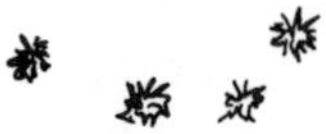

moderate 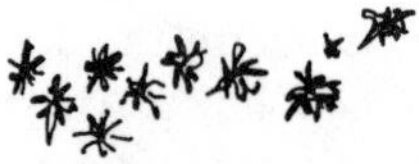

dense 

Campsites

In rating the quality of campsites, we have taken into account the following factors (not necessarily in this order of importance):

view
availability of water
availability of wood
amount of use
ground cover
considerations of safety and comfort: snags, exposure, sun location
considerations of conservation
kind of soil or rock–fireplace danger
mosquito problems
nearby educational and recreational possibilities
degree of remoteness
swimming possibilities
amount of man-made construction
general feel of the area

Maps

The maps in this book are adapted from the 15-minute series of topographic maps prepared by the United States Geological Survey. Where these maps did not show the true situation as we found it in the field, we corrected them. On these maps some peaks are named, but others merely bear a number indicating the elevation, as "8721." When referring to one of these points, we call it, for example, "Peak 8721." The maps that cover the Tahoe-Yosemite Trail are:

Tahoe
Fallen Leaf Lake
Silver Lake
Markleeville
Big Meadow
Dardanelles Cone
Sonora Pass
Tower Peak
Matterhorn Peak
Tuolumne Meadows

Mileage Table

Meeks Bay Trailhead	0.0
Stony Ridge Lake	6.3
Phipps Pass	9.1
Fontanillis Lake	14.2
Dicks Pass	17.0
Lake Aloha	22.7
Haypress Meadows	25.7
Highway 50	32.0
Showers Lake	38.8
Highway 88	43.9
Winnemucca Lake	46.3
4th of July Lake	49.1
Camp Irene	60.9
Mokelumne Wilderness Bndry.	66.8
Lake Alpine	70.2
No. Fk. Stanislaus R.	73.3
Gabbot Meadow	80.0
Woods Gulch	86.7
Clark Fork Road	90.0
Iceberg Meadow	93.7
Clark Fork Meadow	101.3
Highway 108	105.5
Chipmunk Flat	109.4
Kennedy Meadow Resort	114.4
Grouse Creek	118.4
Sheep Camp	122.6
Brown Bear Pass	125.3
Bond Pass	130.6
Tilden Lake	139.4
Macomb Ridge	143.3
Seavey Pass	152.7
Benson Lake Junction	155.2
Benson Pass	161.3
Miller Lake	168.0
Return Creek	171.6
Glen Aulin	179.9
Tuolumne Meadows	185.7

I. MEEKS BAY TO ECHO SUMMIT

This first section of the Tahoe Yosemite Trail lies almost entirely within one of California's best-known wilderness areas, the Desolation Wilderness. Here 63,469 acres are held forever inviolate against man's engines and works except for the very minimum of structures that may be necessary to preserve the area in its pristine state. The terrain here makes up a miniature Sierra Nevada at a slightly lower elevation than the climax of the High Sierra farther south, beyond Yosemite. One main reason for the similarity is that the Desolation Wilderness was glaciated during the last Ice Age, just as the High Sierra was.

The Tahoe-Yosemite Trail in this area is never far from a road, and frequent glimpses of Lake Tahoe along the trail may call forth images of modern man herding up in all-night gambling palaces and looking for blanket space on littered beaches. Yet near the trail one can find many campsites that give a feeling of utter remoteness.

Because this section of the Tahoe-Yosemite Trail is the most accessible of any section, the area offers a wide choice of day walks and overnights that reach or include parts of the Tahoe-Yosemite Trail.

A wooden Forest Service sign across Highway 89 from a parking lot in Meeks Bay proclaims the start of the *Desolation Trail,* though for the first 1 1/3 miles the route follows a dirt road. Here in a forest of white fir, ponderosa pine, lodgepole pine and incense-cedar, the eager hiker hits the trail that can take him 180 miles to Tuolumne Meadows in Yosemite National Park. Under the cool green trees, bracken fern and gooseberry share the fertile soil, and somewhere in the canyon bottom, faintly heard, Meeks Creek carries snow water from the high, white fields down to Lake Tahoe.

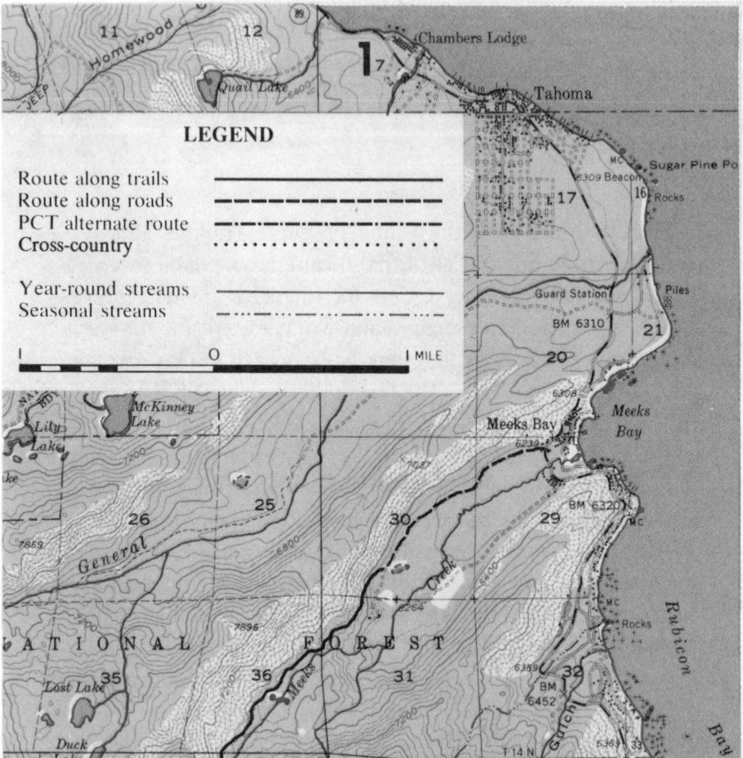

see MAP 2

Soon we begin to see more lodgepole pines, most numerous of all the cone-bearing trees along the Tahoe-Yosemite Trail. About 2 miles from the trailhead the path crosses the boundary of the Desolation Wilderness, beyond which buildings, motorized vehicles, jackhammers and jetports are prohibited. As our moderate ascent continues, we pass a spring where currant bushes and corn lilies thrive, and purple lupine and red paintbrush dominate the slope above. Beyond the spring, the trail levels, and the striking trees beside the trail here are mountain junipers. These rugged trees with thick, sienna-barked trunks are members of the cypress family, and are very unlike the more common needle-bearing conifers of the High Sierra.

The sound of Meeks Creek becomes clear as the trail nears the water, and one wonders whether a mountain stream ever sounded anything but happy, even on its worst days. At a seep here beside the creek, in June or July, you will see a blossoming of paintbrush, monkey flower, columbine and tiger lily. The trail, veering away from the stream, is sandy and level as it passes through a meadow and then a forested, meadowy glade of ferns. It later crosses another meadow, containing a tall, dead two-trunked Jeffrey pine. In season, this meadow is a garden of mule-ear plants, with their large yellow flowers.

The ascent becomes gentle to moderate under a sparse, mixed forest cover, then gives way to a short, moderate-to-steep ascent on a rocky trail section. Along this ascent red fir, sometimes called silvertip, begins to appear. At the ford of Meeks Creek a hundred yards farther on, there is a good campsite. (This boulder ford may be difficult in early season.) To ford Meeks Creek at high water, walk 50 yards upstream from the campsite just before the regular ford, and, while walking on a downed, rotting log, turn left and at the base of the largest lodgepole pine around, find the upper end of a down log that crosses the creek. This log is easy to see from the campsite on the east side of the creek.

Across the ford and 80 yards upstream is another good campsite under lodgepole, white and Jeffrey pine, and red fir. Many pan-size brook and brown trout lie in small holes shaded by thickets of dogwood, alder, willows and mountain ash.

From here the sandy trail steadily ascends the east wall of the canyon, looping away from the creek to gain the height of its steep cascade. On this loop we meet another high-altitude conifer, the mountain hemlock, always distinguished by its gracefully curving tip. Just beyond a waterfall the trail reaches the shore of Lake Genevieve, a shallow, warmish, pine-rimmed, green lake with fair campsites at the north end

see MAP 1

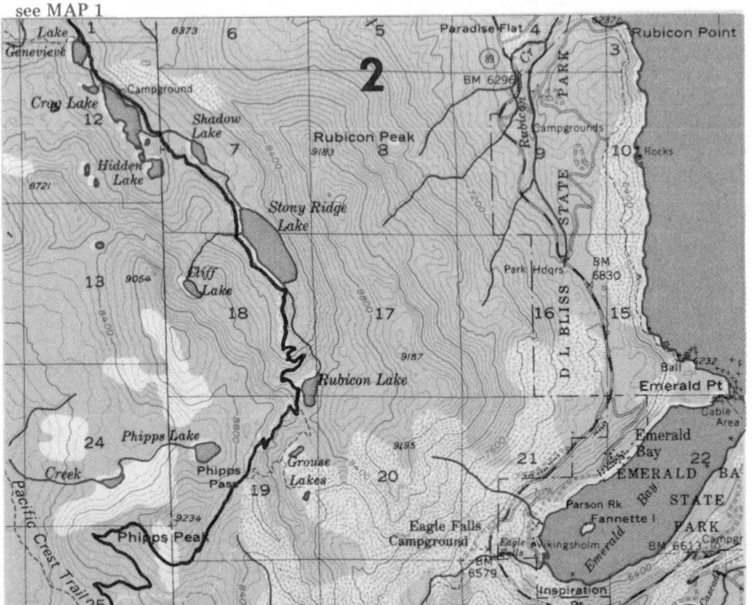

see MAP 3

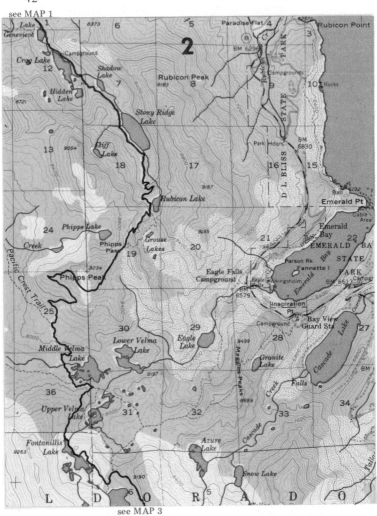

and along the east side. All these campsites look across the water at photogenic Peak 9054. The early riser will be rewarded by the sight of this mountain bathed in sunrise light crowning a mantle of blue shadows. Firewood is scarce. The General Creek trail leads west across the outlet.

From Lake Genevieve to Crag Lake the trail makes a short, gentle ascent under red fir, silver pine and Jeffrey pine. Crag Lake has a flow-maintenance dam at the outlet. Such dams, of which there are scores in the high country, were built by the state Department of Fish and Game, the U.S. Forest Service and private sportsmen's groups. Adequate flow in the stream below is provided by adjustments of the outlet valve during the summer. DF&G biologists and wardens do the adjusting. There are some fair and some good campsites on Crag Lake, along the east side, on the glacial moraine that makes up this side of the lake basin.

Our route now ascends moderately, on rocky underfooting to a boulder ford of Meeks Creek. Just beyond the ford is the junction of a trail to Hidden Lake, and a few yards farther on we see that lake close below through an opening in the trees. This lake maintains a brook-trout population, in spite of increasing use. Veering away from the creek, our trail ascends gently through dense pine forest and passes above meadow-bordered, lily-dotted Shadow Lake. From here, a steady ascent diagonally up a curving moraine, beside rapids and cataracts, brings us to Stony Ridge Lake, the largest of the six lakes (the Tallant Lakes) in this valley, and the only one with rainbow as well as brown trout (and even a few lake trout). There are fair-to-good campsites at the outlet, along the west side, and at the head of the lake. Pines, mostly lodgepole, rim the lake except along the steep eastern shore. A short distance up the rocky western slope, gray-green sagebrush makes the observer question the notion that sagebrush defines desert. At the head of Stony Ridge Lake we take the right-hand fork at an unsigned trail **Y** and make a slight ascent overlooking the green, marshy meadow above the lake. For the next ½ mile the trail is mostly level as it crosses a wet hillside where the flower gardens are the best yet seen on the Tahoe-Yosemite Trail. Flowers are in bloom here until the end of the summer, and they beckon the hiker to rest and admire them. Then we must mount a series of switchbacks that gain 300 feet of elevation. As the trail completes the switchbacks and turns south, it parallels the east side of a small, north-facing glacial cirque. Black, lichen-streaked cliffs stand 200 feet high above a talus-block fan. Listen for the "eenk" sound of conies scuttering about in the talus, storing the grass they have dried to sustain them over the winter. In early season the wide, sweeping snowbank in this cirque, stained red by millions of minute algae, is a small reminder of the glacier that sculpted the curving head-wall before us. Soon we arrive at the crowning jewel of the Tallant Lakes, Rubicon Lake, which has several excellent campsites watched over by a wealth of those birds called Clark nutcrackers. These high-altitude "camp robbers" swoop back and forth across the lake, exchanging perches in the lodgepole and hemlock that surround the clear, green-tinted water, waiting for you to leave a bird's meal in your camp.

A hundred yards up the cool, shaded trail is a lateral trail to Grouse Lakes, to the left. Then, after two switchbacks, we look down into the gray-green valley of Eagle Falls Creek and across it to the snow-covered north slope of Mt. Tallac. This rocky portion of the trail ascends moderately and then levels off somewhat to traverse along the side of the ridge overlooking Grouse Lakes and the Eagle Falls drainage. Taking a breather stop, we can see Cascade Lake and Fallen Leaf Lake, reminding us how few steps are needed to put us into this wilderness. Where the route to Phipps Lake departs to the right, the traverse gives way to a set of Forest Service steps—6 x 6 milled lumber held in place by steel pegs. This recently constructed trail section is different from the route shown on the topo map. The new trail passes above the saddle where the trail leading south from Grouse Lakes is shown intersecting the main trail. For some reason the new section contours around the south side of Phipps Peak until it is headed almost due north, at which point the hiker might begin to worry, knowing that he wants to go to the Velma Lakes. He will.

At the highest trail point on this slope of Phipps Peak, handsome Dicks Peak comes into view, and some peaks of the Crystal Range are visible over its right shoulder. Having been in gray granite country since the beginning of the journey, we are struck by the reddish-brown metasedimentary rocks of Dicks Peak and its outliers.

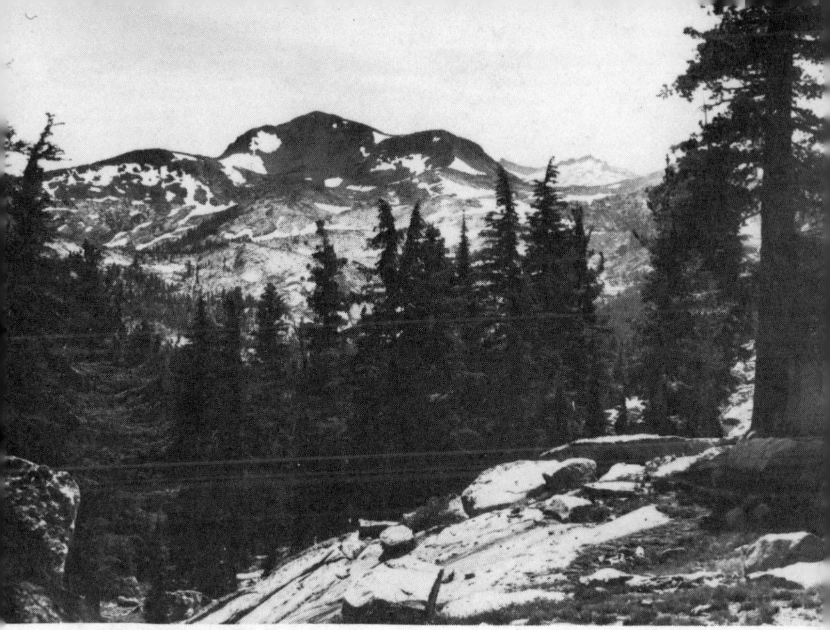

Dicks Peak from Phipps Pass

A short distance farther, we come into sight of all three Velma Lakes at once. These lakes, named for a daughter of Nevada mining king Harry Comstock, lie close together in a single basin—but Upper and Lower Velma lakes drain into Lake Tahoe and ultimately into Nevada, while Middle Velma drains into the Rubicon River and ultimately into the Pacific Ocean. From this vantage point the experienced knapsacker may wish to head cross-country straight for Middle Velma Lake, because the Tahoe-Yosemite Trail route to there is quite indirect.

Our trail veers westward, and we have excellent views of the northern part of the Crystal Range, including Rockbound Pass—the deepest notch visible—and the basins of Lakes Lois and Schmidell. These landmarks are in sight for a mile or more as the trail, departing from the topo-map indication, circles around the north side of Phipps Peak until it is north of the "h" in "Phipps Pass." Finally, at a hairpin turn, the trail heads back toward Velma Lakes. A few yards northwest of this turn is a viewpoint overlooking much of Rockbound

see MAP 2

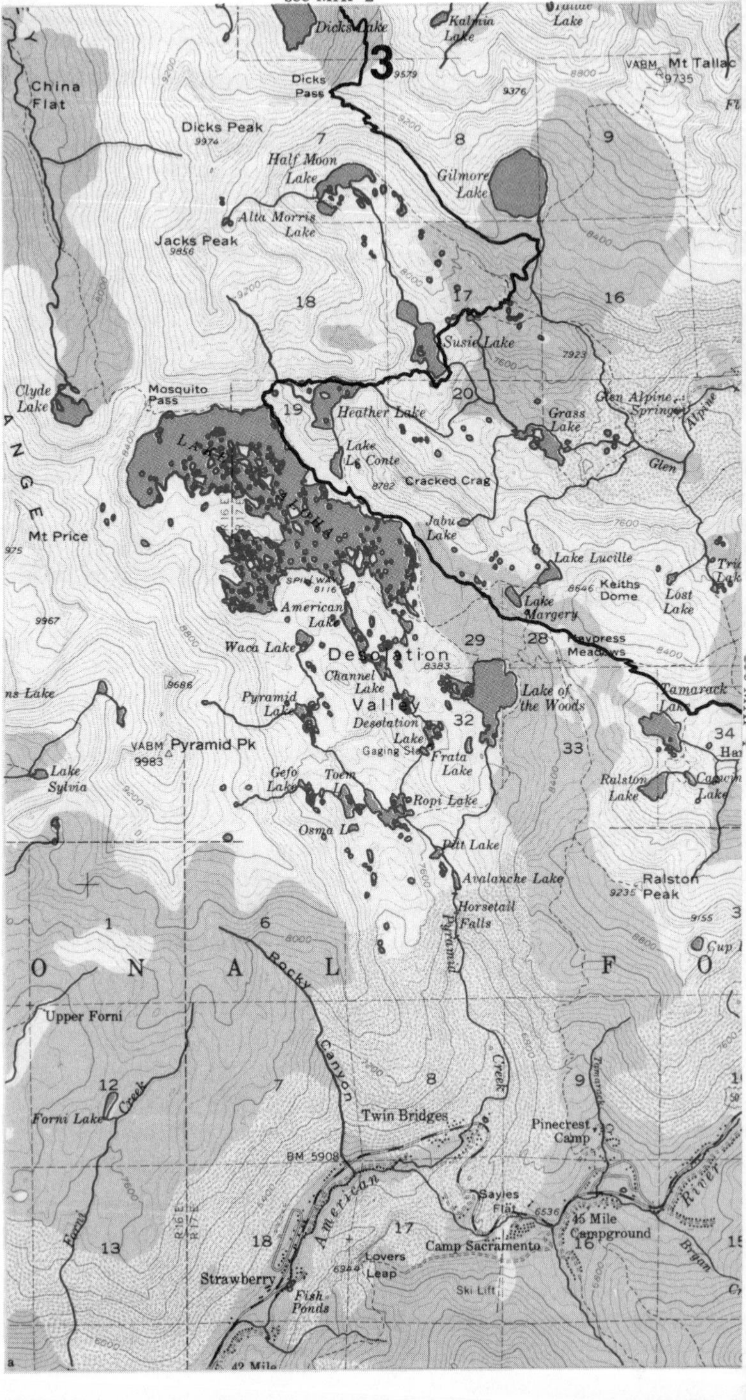

Dicks Lake
Kalmia Lake
Tallac Lake
3
Mt Tallac
9735
Dicks Pass
China Flat
Dicks Peak
9974
Half Moon Lake
Gilmore Lake
Alta Morris Lake
Jacks Peak
9856
Susie Lake
Glen Alpine Springs
Clyde Lake
Mosquito Pass
Heather Lake
Grass Lake
Lake Le Conte
Cracked Crag
Lake Aloha
Mt Price
Jabu Lake
Lake Lucille
Keiths Dome
Lost Lake
Lake Margery
American Lake
Haypress Meadows
Waca Lake
Desolation Valley
Channel Lake
Lake of the Woods
Tamarack Lake
Pyramid Lake
Desolation Lake
Gaging Sta
VABM Pyramid Pk
9983
Lake Sylvia
Frata Lake
Gefo Lake
Toem L
Ropi Lake
Ralston Lake
Osma L
Pitt Lake
Avalanche Lake
Horsetail Falls
Ralston Peak
9235
Cup L
Upper Forni
Rocky Canyon
Pyramid Creek
Forni Lake
Forni Creek
Twin Bridges
Pinecrest Camp
BM 5908
Sayles Flat
45 Mile Campground
American River
Camp Sacramento
Lovers Leap
Strawberry
Fish Ponds
Ski Lift
42 Mile

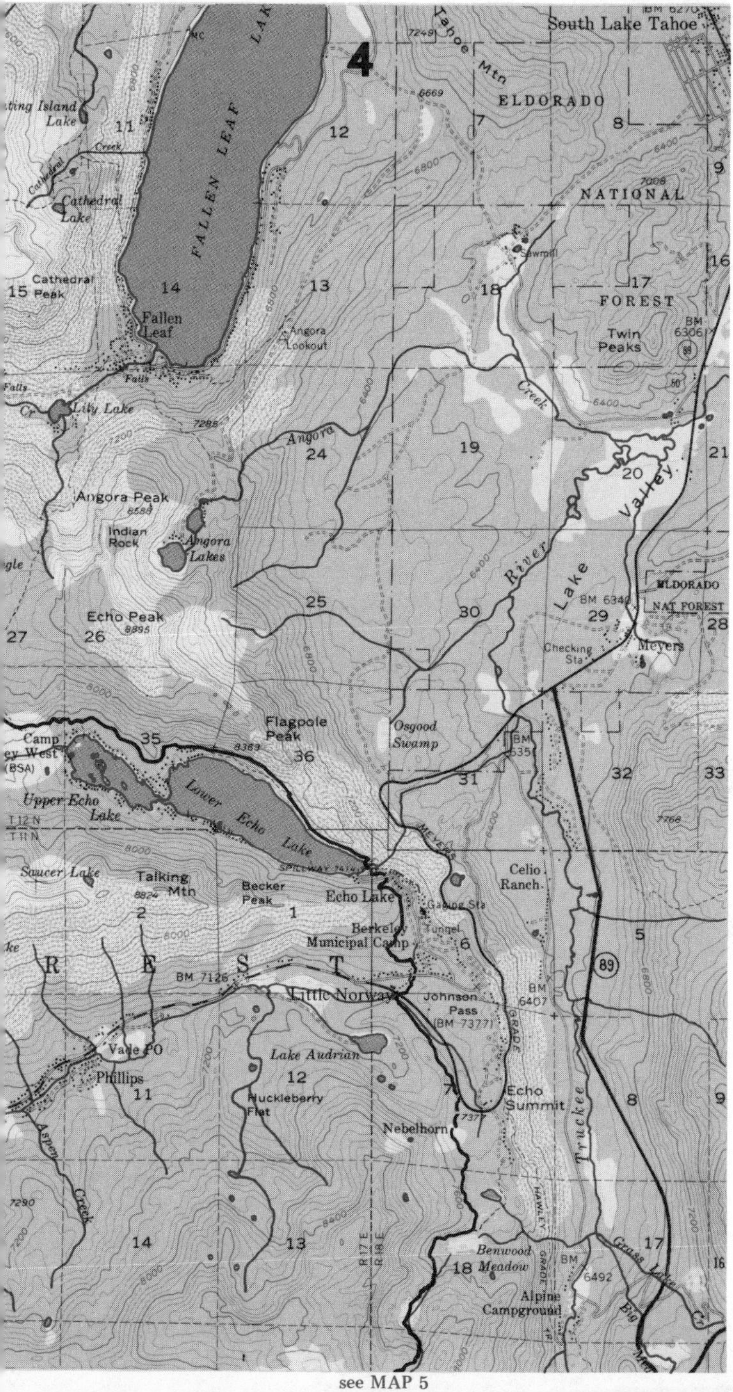
4
South Lake Tahoe
Tahoe Mtn
ELDORADO
NATIONAL
FOREST
FALLEN LEAF LAKE
Lake
11
12
7
8
9
Creek
Cathedral
Cathedral Lake
Cathedral Peak
15
14
13
18
17
16
Sawmill
Fallen Leaf
Falls
Angora Lookout
Twin Peaks
BM 6306
Lily Lake
Cr
Angora
24
19
Creek
20
21
Valley
Lake
Angora Peak
8588
Indian Rock
Angora Lakes
River
25
30
29
28
BM 6340
ELDORADO NAT FOREST
Echo Peak
8895
27
26
Checking Sta
Meyers
Camp
(BSA)
35
Flagpole Peak
8383
36
Osgood Swamp
31
32
33
Upper Echo Lake
Lower Echo Lake
T 12 N
T 11 N
SPILLWAY 7414
Saucer Lake
Talking Mtn
8824
Becker Peak
Echo Lake
2
1
Gaging Sta
Celio Ranch.
Berkeley Municipal Camp
Tunnel
6
5
89
R
E
S
T
BM 7126
Little Norway
Johnson Pass
(BM 7377)
BM 6407
Vade PO
Phillips
11
Lake Audrian
12
Huckleberry Flat
Echo Summit
7377
Nebelhorn
Truckee
8
9
Aspen
Creek
7290
14
13
R 17 E
R 18 E
Benwood Meadow
18
BM 6492
17
Alpine Campground
Grass Lake
Big
16

see MAP 5

Valley, including Rockbound Lake, which lies at the northwest corner of the wilderness area. Here we begin a steady, sandy descent of several miles including three long switchback legs. We pass through a moderate-to-dense forest cover of red fir, interspersed with some silver pine, lodgepole and hemlock, and arrive at the junction of the Pacific Crest Trail. From here to Middle Velma Lake, our route wanders more than seems necessary, finally passing a trail to Camper Flat on the Rubicon River just before we hop over a sluggish creek.

At the southwest end of forested Middle Velma Lake, the Tahoe-Yosemite Trail skirts a cove and rises above the lake into a red-fir forest. On many north-facing slopes like this one, red fir forms a thick, dark forest where a few shade-tolerant plants make a sparse ground cover. We see many fallen trees and parts of trees, downed by winter storms—red fir is more vulnerable to breakage than any other Sierra conifer. On the forest floor we see the ragged cores of fir cones that remain after a chickaree's meal of cone seeds. The Sierra chickaree climbs the fir in the fall to cut green cones. He caches these, and the cold keeps them fresh until he is ready to eat them. If a chickaree does not fell the cone, it will, unlike a pine cone, disintegrate on the tree.

The shady duff trail soon arrives at a junction, where it turns right toward Dicks Pass. The junction is not shown on the topo map; it is about 200 yards west of the map junction that lies between Middle and Upper Velma lakes. One may choose to camp here, or follow the old trail up the west side of Upper Velma Lake to the good campsites at the inlet. In a meadow of sedge and corn lilies where the old trail first touches Upper Velma Lake, one can see "ropes" of soil that are the sign of the pocket gopher. During the winter he tunnels in the snow to eat the above-ground parts of plants. Later, when he tunnels in the earth, he fills the snow tunnels with the extracted dirt. When the snow melts, these casts descend to the ground to lie where we find them.

From the new junction not shown on the map, the Tahoe-Yosemite Trail ascends south on a moderate grade overlooking Upper Velma Lake. As the slope decreases to gentle, there are views of Dicks Pass and of Lake Tahoe, and then, close ahead, of Fontanillis Lake. After descending gently for a short distance, we cross the lake's outlet. This lake, in a rocky basin dominated by Dicks Peak, offers fair campsites in little stands of lodgepole and hemlock, and a lavish display of red and sienna rocks to complement the familiar granite grays. Leaving Fontanillis, the sandy trail ascends a bouldery granite hillside with several meltwater tarns that could offer a fine swim at just the right time of year. At the top of this rise we meet the short lateral to Dicks Lake. This cirque lake close under Dicks Peak has several fair campsites and one good one on its timbered eastern shore, plus a self-sustaining brook-trout population. At the junction, the Tahoe-Yosemite Trail turns left, and proceeds a short distance to another junction in a saddle overlooking the drainage of Eagle Falls Creek to the east. Standing at this junction, marked by a cairn, we see other cairns indicating the route to the south. From here, the rocky trail ascends steadily on a granite slope sparsely dotted with lodgepole. Far below, a large area of downed trees

Upper Velma Lake

on the southwest slope of the Dicks Lake cirque gives evidence of an avalanche.

Our trail steepens, sometimes going straight up slopes of decomposed granite ("gruss") which might be better negotiated via switchbacks. This steep slope is usually snow-covered into July. Several unsigned but well-ducked trails take off from our route, and one should resist their blandishments. This dry (except in early season) ascent ends at Dicks Pass (9380′), which is somewhat east of the actual low point of the divide.

Standing at the pass with pack off and shoulders recuperating, the backpacker can survey a considerable part of California, from Sierra Buttes, beyond Yuba Pass in the north, to Round Top, beyond Carson Pass in the south. Closer in the south, Pyramid Peak rises above Lake Aloha, and from just beyond the pass we can see Susie and Grass lakes in the wooded basin of Glen Alpine Creek. The sign at the pass stands at the center of several almost flat acres, strewn with the rocky products of erosion. (Such an area is in fact called "erosion pavement.") All the trees here are whitebark pines, the high-

Looking south from Dicks Pass

est-dwelling conifer we will encounter on the Tahoe-Yosemite Trail. There are good campsites east of the pass—when snow-melt provides water.

Descending from the "pass" to the actual saddle, we can see Half Moon Lake to the south, and we look back on Fontanillis and Dicks lakes. The trail is now on the warm, south-facing slope, and when there is still much snow on the north side, the southern switchbacks display a springtime show of paint-brush, sulfur flower, white heather, western wallflower, white and lavender phlox, and elderberry. At the saddle on this divide, a trail of use leaves the main trail to ascend nearby Dicks Peak. A few hundred feet from the saddle is a very large whitebark pine beside the trail. Unlike the trees at the pass, this one has no visible white bark, the bark having assumed its mature, dark form. From here, our trail traverses gently down the side of a ridge toward Gilmore Lake. Along this traverse the variety of wildflowers multiplies almost with every step. At the height of the blossoming season, one may see delphinium, deerbrush, spiraea, creamberry, red heather, buckwheat, groundsel, serviceberry, corn lily, penstemon, white heather, pussy paws and buttercups. At about the elevation of the first red firs, we pass the trail to Gilmore Lake (good campsites, three species of trout) and Mt. Tallac, and begin a switchbacking descent through a mixed forest cover. (For an unsurpassed view of the Tahoe basin, spend half a day to climb Mt. Tallac.)

Soon we pass a junction whence a faint lateral trail leads right to Half Moon Lake and a more prominent one goes left to Glen Alpine Spring. Our route continues down a rocky trail toward Susie Lake. In a swampy, flowery meadow ½ mile later we pass another trail to Glen Alpine and Fallen Leaf Lake. From it, a moderate, short, winding ascent brings us to the rise overlooking Susie Lake, one of the most used lakes in this wilderness area. Campsites are poor to fair here. Beyond the lake's outlet, a difficult ford in early season, a trail leads down the canyon to large, forested campsites.

We continue around the shore for a while, and then climb steadily up to the **V** at the outlet of the Heather Lake basin, formed by the slopes of Jacks Peak on the north and Cracked Crag on the south. (In early season there is always snow here.) On the slope of Jacks Peak is a clear line of division between the metasedimentary rock of the "Mt. Tallac pendant" and the gray granite south of it. Our route follows a rocky course well above Heather Lake, leading over a small ridge and then just above a placid tarn. To find the best campsites at this lake, walk down beside the last main inlet stream. Alternatively, there are good campsites beside a tarn that lies just below the headwall of the Heather Lake cirque. Heather Lake has rainbow, brook and some large brown trout.

The short, rocky climb from the campsites above Heather Lake to Desolation Valley itself surmounts a divide where we have a magnificent close-up of the Crystal Range. Rising above the far shore of shallow Lake Aloha, this classic range is a superb glacial ridge left standing high after moving ice on both sides of it plucked immense quantities of rock from its flanks and carried them away downslope. Parts of the ridge line are like a knife edge—what geologists call an arête—and the snowfields at the base of the knife blade look like glaciers still. As the ice rivers retreated, the forests and meadows advanced to clothe the moraines, the rock-rimmed basins and the rugged cliffs. And along with plants came the animal life—the mammals and birds, the reptiles, amphibians and insects.

It is worth camping somewhere along here to watch the morning sun turn the Crystal Range from blue-gray to gold. Foregrounding Mt. Price, Pyramid Peak and the peaks between is a blue sheet of water over two miles long, dotted with a thousand granite islands on some of which there is just a single weatherbeaten lodgepole snag.

Where we come to the edge of Lake Aloha, the trail to Mosquito Pass and Rockbound Valley leads west, but we turn southeast along the shore, where we find barren granite polished by the old glaciers. After ½ mile we turn and immediately reach a flat where we encounter a junction—usually snowbound till late July—with the spur trail to Lake LeConte. This lake has several small, fair campsites on the east side.

Pyramid Peak and Peak 9686

Even in this "Desolation Valley," formerly called "Devils Basin," life is plentiful. Coyotes are often heard and sometimes seen, and yellow-bellied marmots virtually infest the talus slopes of Cracked Crag. Water snakes and skinks fill their ecological niches. The bountiful crop of wildflowers includes white heather, Douglas phlox, buckwheat, groundsel, paintbrush, mountain penstemon, stonecrop, streptanthus, pennyroyal and buttercups. Besides lodgepole pine, there are mountain hemlock, silver pine, red fir, and juniper. Lake Aloha itself has thousands of brook and rainbow trout.

As the trail approaches forest cover, we veer left at a junction where going straight ahead would take one to Lake of the Woods. The forest cover is sparse, with meadows among the stands of lodgepole. Hundreds of small lodgepole trees in these meadows illustrate the invasion that eventually eradicates every Sierra meadow. The deep ruts of the trail facilitate the takeover—as does anything that pierces the thick turf enough to allow a lodgepole seed to get its roots into the dirt.

After a short ascent, we come to a highly scenic area where many tarns, in early to mid season, reflect the green pines and hemlocks and the house-size gray boulders brought here by the glacier. Near the westernmost tarn the trail to Lakes Margery and Lucille leads off to the east, to good campsites on both lakes, and to bearably warm swimming. In a short quarter mile a well-used trail from Lake Aloha merges with ours. Then, 1/3 mile farther is another junction, where the southern trail from Lake Lucille meets our route. The excavated level place beside this junction once held a log cabin used by trail crews and others needing emergency shelter.

About two hundred yards beyond, we pass on the right a trail to Lake of the Woods and in another 350 yards, another such trail. Our wide, sandy, level trail passes above Haypress Meadows, which boasts one of the largest expanses of grass on the Tahoe-Yosemite Trail. This grass was once harvested for sale to wagon trains crossing Echo Summit. As we pass an abandoned trail, Echo Lake comes into view down the valley

Lake Lucille Trail Junction

Looking down Echo Lake

of Echo Creek. Here the trail steepens and becomes rocky. A trail veers left up the hill, leading to Lily Lake and Fallen Leaf Lake. Over the left shoulder of Talking Mountain we see in the distance the peak with the conical top that we first saw even before reaching Phipps Pass–Hawkins Peak, east of Carson Pass. At the last switchback of a series, there are rocks and logs to sit on, water and shade. Leaving here, the would-be botanist can recognize the first pine tree straight ahead down-trail as a silver (western white) pine, by the many thin brown cones in twos and threes hanging from the tips of its high branches.

We now begin a long traverse down a moderately graded, rock-filled trail. The hiker should be especially careful with his footing on this trail bed of loose granite. Even though many daywalkers and horseback riders come up here, it is hard to see the justification for the extensive blasting and grading of this trail section, which some have called a "freeway."

Beyond a junction with the Tamarack Lake lateral, we re-enter forest–a heavy cover of lodgepole, later thinning somewhat and showing inclusions of Jeffrey pine. Beyond the forest another unsigned trail to the Fallen Leaf Lake area goes left up the hill, and in 300 yards we leave Desolation Wilderness. Soon we come to one of several short laterals leading to Camp Harvey West and the boat-taxi landing at the upper end of Echo Lake.

The trail from Camp Harvey West to the Echo Lakes Resort skirts the north side of Upper and Lower Echo lakes. The 3-mile walk is unremarkable, and can be avoided by taking the commercial boat-taxi from Camp Harvey West to the chalet. One can telephone for a boat from the phone booth near the camp's pier. If, however, one chooses to "walk it out," one can expect a wide and well-trod trail that goes discouragingly high above the lake. The final portion is on a dusty, exposed, south-facing slope, making the walk uncomfortably warm in the afternoon.

After a milk shake or other morale-booster at Echo Lake Resort, walk up the road to the large upper parking lot and on the west edge of it find a segment of Pacific Crest Trail/Tahoe-Yosemite Trail constructed in 1978. This segment first makes a long switchback leg westward before turning east to climb gently through red firs above many summer-home cabins. Then it veers first south, then southwest and finally southeast before reaching, about 1 mile from its start, a blacktop road, which it crosses about ½ mile west of Johnson Pass.

Across the blacktop road, proceed south on the duff trail through a heavy forest cover of Jeffrey and lodgepole pine and red fir. In a few minutes you emerge at Highway 50 just east of the establishment called Little Norway. Cross the highway here and on the south side find a resumption of your trail as it turns east to parallel the highway toward Echo Summit. In a short mile this section ends at the blacktop entrance road of a small downhill skiing area.

II. ECHO SUMMIT TO CARSON PASS

This section of the Tahoe-Yosemite Trail has attractions far greater than its reputation. In fact, it hardly has a reputation. Few people mention it; one can walk the whole section in midsummer and not see a soul. For an area bordered by an all-year U.S. highway and an all-year state highway, that is an incredible amount of non-use. One reason may be the wise decision by the Forest Service to close most of the area to vehicular travel. Maps of the closure may be obtained from the Service in San Francisco or Placerville (see Appendix). The hiker can help the Forest Service enforce these regulations by reporting to it the license number of any vehicle he sees in a closed area.

From the small ski area near Echo Summit, the Tahoe-Yosemite Trail ascends diagonally south-east up ski slopes until it is beyond this area of tree massacre. Then, swinging south, we stroll along granite-dotted slopes covered by white firs and lodgepole and Jeffrey pines, with a generous understory of huckleberry oak bushes. Soon we descend to the portals of Benwood Meadow, where the pre-1978 trail comes in from the left. Along the wet margins of this meadow, the flower-spotter will have his eyes full checking the aster, corn lily, snow plant, alpine lily, monkey flower, penstemon, false solomon's seal, squawroot, pennyroyal, groundsel, columbine, larkspur and mountain bluebell, to say nothing of the ferns, grasses and sedges.

Nearing the inflow to the meadow, the trail begins to rise moderately. Then, as the ascent steepens, juniper and mountain hemlock join the forest cover of red fir, silver pine and lodgepole pine. At the top of the steep slope, the trail fords a runoff stream and levels off on duff underfooting as it approaches another meadow.

The trail around the west side of this meadow is indistinct, but our route can be picked up again in the shadow of a 70-foot granite cliff at the south end of the meadow, near the main inlet stream. There is a good campsite on this stream, where the quiet camper may set up an observation post to study the wildlife that passes here.

Leaving this meadow, the Tahoe-Yosemite Trail climbs steeply beneath moderate-to-dense red fir. After a few hundred yards the trail levels as it passes a small, willowy meadow, and then it commences an extremely steep series of switchbacks up a granitic slope, which can be snowbound and treacherous until mid-July. In a flowery bowl at the head of the stream drainage we have been ascending, just below a last willow-covered slope, ford the stream and again pick up the trail. After a few feet of steep ascent, the grade eases, then the route levels off on the east shoulder of Peak 8905 and heads southward.

Here the plant life changes as we reach a southern exposure, hemlock giving way to lodgepole pine, and sagebrush making its first appearance for many miles. Through clearings in these trees the walker has views to the southeast of Stevens Peak, Red Lake Peak, Elephants Back and Round Top. The

see MAP 4

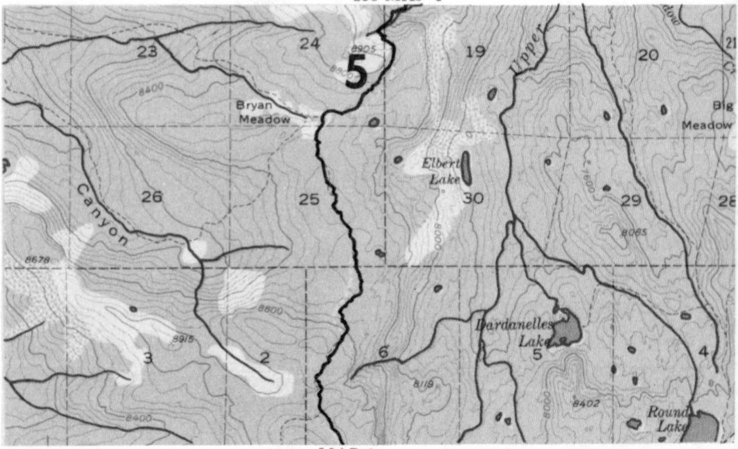

see MAP 6

Roots of fallen lodgepole near Sayles Canyon

strong layering on the sides of Stevens and Red Lake is evidence of the volcanic flows that piled atop one another to create these eminences.

On this southern slope our sandy trail descends gently to moderately through meadowy slopes dotted with wildflowers. When the trail reaches a gully, we follow it west over a low saddle and descend it 200 yards to a junction in Bryan Meadow. There are several campsites here, and water is plentiful in early season.

From Bryan Meadow the trail leads south on sandy footing, undulating and then ascending gently to a minor summit. Then it makes a brief descent to a saddle from where the Sayles Canyon Trail descends southwest to Round Meadow and then northwest down to Highway 50. Less than a mile after this junction, the trail makes a short, steep ascent up over the east ridge of a 9000-foot unnamed peak which separates the two branches of the headwaters of Sayles Canyon Creek.

At the first saddle beyond the ridge, a trail of use (not on the topographic map) crosses our trail at right angles, and a short distance farther on we come to the junction with the trail to Schneider's cow camp. Then we head straight across a willow-covered meadow, finding the trail again on the far side of it.

Beyond this meadow, the character of the rocks begins to change from granitic to volcanic, and the sand we are treading turns pinkish. Here we begin a descent into a large bowl whose southwest rim is for most of the summer draped with snow cornices. The slopes of this bowl are very open, laced with runoff streams, and lavishly planted with bushes and flowers: blue elderberry, swamp whiteheads, mountain bluebells, green gentian, aster, wallflower, penstemon, several species of cinquefoil, spiraea, corn lily and columbine. This highly colorful bowl, containing Showers Lake, offers the photographer a great choice of hues, subjects and compositions.

In this bowl, the trail makes a gentle descent to pass beneath a palisade-like outcropping below the cornice-laden rim of the bowl. Before you can see Showers Lake, the trail veers northeast, and eventually it drops below the lake to cross the lake's outlet stream. You have two choices besides follow-

The bowl northwest of Showers Lake

see MAP 5

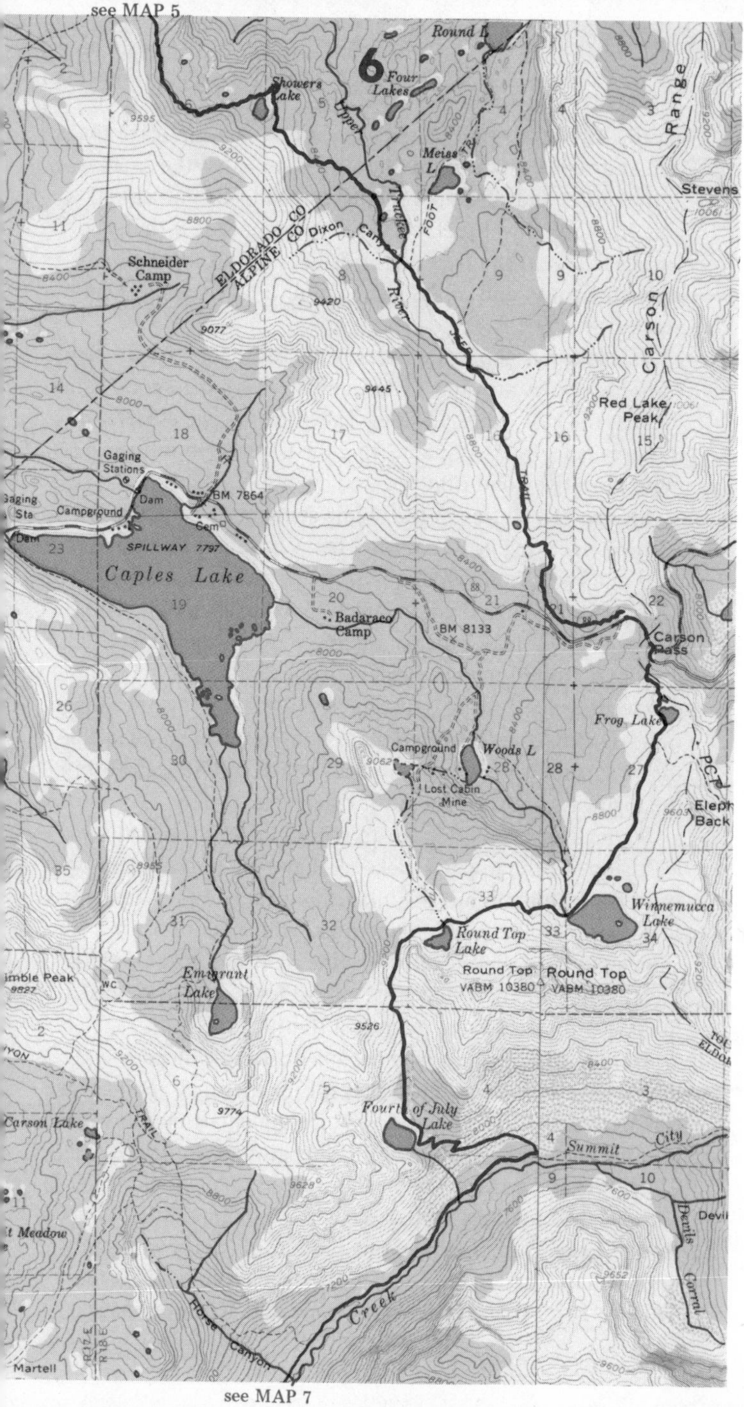

see MAP 7

ing this circuitous trail all the way. First, you can leave the trail and strike eastward to Showers Lake, cross the small dam at the outlet and find the trail just beyond. Or you can, if you don't mind wet feet, cross the boggy meadow that you see ahead just as the trail veers northeast. This meadow is above the south end of the lake, and until late season is very mucky.

This lake has good campsites at the south end, with a few whitebark pines at water's edge, and several fair-to-good campsites on the east, forested side. The 1969 vehicle closure in this area is fortunately permitting the lakeside to return to a more primitive condition.

From a blazed tree in the saddle southeast of the lake we follow a decaying jeep trail for a few yards, and then turn right at a fork, from which the route leads down another slope having vegetation and colors much like the last bowl. This trail segment offers some panoramic views of the large meadows around the headwaters of the Truckee River. Should one want a clue for the best time to walk here, this meadowy valley is at its greatest when there is just a bit of snow left on the west side of the Crystal Range—which can be seen from the highway a few miles east of Placerville.

We make a steady descent to rejoin the jeep road on the west slope of the upper Truckee Valley. Many trails veer right from the jeep road, but the hiker should stay on it. Just north of a river ford, the northbound hiker will encounter a **Y** choice point. Take the left fork; the right one goes to Meiss Lake, which can be seen across almost level ground if one looks northward from a point just south of the ford.

During the Ice Age a lake occupied all these meadows. It has been filled with sediment except for the small remnant we call Meiss Lake. These meadows offer much attraction for the bird-watcher, and also for the Belding ground squirrel fancier. The house and barn in the meadow are used by stockmen.

Near the buildings we pass a signed junction with the Round Lake Trail, and then our route fords the river again and begins a last, moderate ascent to the saddle that divides the Truckee River drainage from the American River drainage.

A few hundred yards north of the saddle, the northbound traveler will turn left at a choice point; to a southbound walker the route is obvious. As we near the saddle, we have increasingly fine views of the Round Top complex of peaks a few miles off in the south, and the view from the saddle itself is panoramic.

From this saddle our route descends steeply on a rocky-dusty jeep road (which is now closed to vehicles and is reverting to trail) for several hundred yards to a junction, where the jeep road continues south and the Tahoe-Yosemite Trail turns east. The trail makes a few switchbacks down through mule ears and sagebrush, crosses a runoff stream, and then curves around the nose of a ridge through a moderate forest cover of pine and fir. Soon you can hear the cars on Highway 88 not far below you, but the trail refuses to meet the highway halfway, and it takes longer than you expect to finally reach the parking lot one-third mile west of Carson Pass.

Edge of Meiss Meadows

III. CARSON PASS TO LAKE ALPINE

This section of the Tahoe-Yosemite Trail begins and ends on high-speed highways, but in between it leads through a little-used part of the trail, in the canyon of the Mokelumne River.

A few hour's walk from Carson Pass the trail enters the Mokelumne Wilderness, a region of 50,450 acres where only foot travel is permitted. At the border one begins the long descent to the crossing of the Mokelumne River, the lowest point on the Tahoe-Yosemite Trail (5200′). Beyond the river is the toughest climb on the whole trail. But the exertion is repaid by the delights of Summit City canyon, and the big brown trout in the Mokelumne River, the swimming in the flowing waters and the scarcity of people.

Upon reaching Highway 88, the Tahoe-Yosemite Trail veers east to Carson Pass and then goes 100 yards down the old highway to the signed trail to Lake Winnemucca. From here, it makes a short, rocky climb of half a mile, gaining 300 feet elevation, to a plateau that contains Frog Lake, where the view of Round Top and nearby peaks seen from north of the pass is recaptured. Somewhere on this plateau John C. Fremont made the first winter crossing of the Sierra, in February 1844, with Kit Carson as his scout. From an excampment in Faith Valley a few miles to the east, Fremont climber Red Lake Peak, just north of Carson Pass, and from the summit he saw the great mountain lake we now call Tahoe. Fremont's diary entry is the first recorded mention of Lake Tahoe, and the climb of Red Lake Peak is the first recorded ascent of an identifiable Sierra peak.

The domelike red prominence immediately to the south is Elephants Back. Large red-tailed hawks are often seen soaring on the thermals that rise up the sides of this dome. Farther ahead is Round Top, which has large snowfields on its north side all year long. At Frog Lake the trail leaves silver and lodgepole pine behind, and enters an area of whitebark pine, juniper and mountain hemlock. The stands of high-altitude-loving whitebark provide nesting places for hundreds of Clark nutcrackers, which swoop back and forth over the hiker passing here. As the Indians did, these birds eat an abundance of whitebark-pine nuts. The fondness of the Clark nutcracker for whitebark-pine nuts is probably one of the main reasons that whitebarks move upward in elevation. Messy eaters, the large, crowlike, gray and white birds drop seeds while picking the cones apart, thus starting new pines.

From Frog Lake, we stroll along a verdant hillside where wildflower gardens are gorgeous in early summer, Sierra birds abound, and views are panoramic. After 1½ miles a gentle descent brings us to the shore of deep, blue Lake Winnemucca, with a few fair campsites on the north side, but no firewood. Stoves may soon be required here. At the outlet, the trail forks, the right fork leading down to a trailhead at Woods Lake. The Tahoe-Yosemite Trail follows the left fork for 1 mile over a little saddle to Round Top Lake. Near this saddle, one has views of a tiny bit of Lake Tahoe (the first view that the northbound traveler on the Tahoe-Yosemite Trail will have of his destination). This stretch of trail, in its spring season, bears rare specimens of a low-growing red-purple flower called rockfringe by laymen, and *Epilobium obcordatum* by Latinizers. More common here are lupine, red heather, penstemon and Douglas phlox. At the outlet of Round Top Lake (many good campsites) the Tahoe-Yosemite Trail crosses a lateral trail leading to Lost Cabin and Woods Lake, and begins its circle around the northwest shoulder of Round Top peak. On the far side of Round Top Lake, the steep cliff is a melange of grays, greens and browns, and the talus slopes vary in color according to which bedrock yielded up which talus blocks. Along this stretch of trail, views are excellent (scanning from east to north to west) of Markleeville Peak, Hawkins Peak, the Crystal Range, and the green-clad slopes of upper Caples Creek.

All the rock outcroppings in this region are dark-colored. Volcanic rocks are normally dark, but even the granite here is much darker than the shining granites in Desolation Valley.

Soon our trail descends to a saddle which is on the border of the Mokelumne Wilderness. Here the Tahoe-Yosemite Trail leaves the basin of the American River and enters the Mokelumne River drainage. Here also we begin the 4000-foot descent to the Mokelumne River crossing, the lowest point on the Tahoe-Yosemite Trail.

Once we begin the Mokelumne descent, it is many miles before we see again four living things that especially characterize the walk from Carson Pass: Clark nutcrackers, red-tailed hawks, whitebark pines and mountain hemlocks. Our trail descends steeply down 1 mile on dusty, decomposed granite to Fourth of July Lake, where there are good campsites around the shore. Unfortunately this lake is overused, and I suggest you continue down to Summit City Creek to camp.

East of the outlet of Fourth of July Lake, our trail turns left and begins a gentle-to-moderate traversing descent into steep-walled Summit City canyon. The timber cover of silver pine, red fir and lodgepole pine soon fades out, and the sandy trail winds among granite outcroppings, heading eastward toward the unnamed pyramidal peak at the head of Summit City canyon. This peak, marked 9381′ on the topo map, is right on the Sierra crest. Where our trail begins to level off, it enters a cover of sparse red fir and lodgepole, which rises above sagebrush, snow bush, creamberry and spiraea.

At the canyon bottom we meet the Summit City canyon trail, and turn right onto it. A few hundred yards west is the site of "lower Summit City," a meadow where only some topped lodgepoles remain to give testimony to man's former settlement. From here our trail descends gently under a cover of dense lodgepole, passing a very built-up campsite. The sandy footpath then begins to descend steadily, the forest cover becomes moderate to sparse, and we begin to see a few yellow pines alongside the lodgepole and red fir. Where the trail crosses open slopes, the hiker has excellent views of the granite walls towering 2000 feet and more above him. Green

Round Top Lake

Fourth of July Lake

see MAP 6

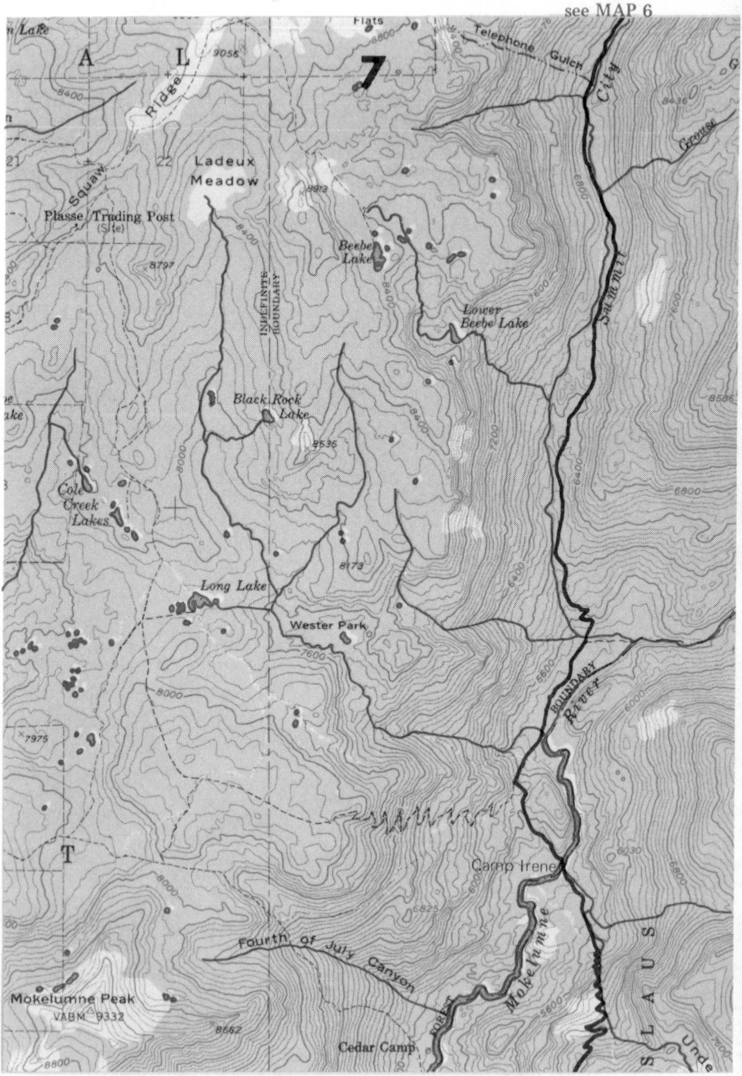

see MAP 8

fingers of brush poke upward between granite outcroppings, and the black color of lichen on the granite reminds the hiker of the same aspect on the walls of Yosemite Valley.

As the trail re-enters a moderate forest cover, some white fir appears along with the red fir, lodgepole and yellow pine, and occasional aspen. Just beyond the Horse Canyon Trail junction we come to the Horse Canyon stream, and several fair-to-good campsites. There are numerous campsites along the main stream in the next mile and a half. About 100 yards beyond the sign *Grouse Creek,* roughly at the point where the trail on the topo map ends, is a fine campsite very close to the creek–too close to be legal.

From here to the Mokelumne River, the essentially cross-country route is variously marked, and sometimes more clear, sometimes less, but at worst you will be delayed in your passage; you can't get lost. You should cross Summit City Creek about 200 yards downstream from the illegal campsite, at a point where deep, narrow channels in the bedrock can contain all the stream flow except in early season, and immediately scramble up the east slope before veering south to parallel the stream. You will go behind a knoll about 30 feet high with a small Jeffrey pine on it, and then proceed parallel to the creek but separated from it by a series of rocky prominences. From time to time ducks give some guidance, as do a few remaining

The Mokelumne Canyon

orange plastic ribbons tied by trail surveyors when the Forest Service intended to construct a trail here.

About ½ mile from the main stream crossing, we dip down beside a very small stream and parallel it for ½ mile, then cross it and contour high on a red-fir-shaded hillside, looking down on a green, aspen-dotted flat where Summit City Creek meanders south. After a little bushwhacking through willow thickets, we descend on open granite to an almost flat area near the stream, then on a fallen log cross a tributary that runs till late summer. After penetrating more brush, we again descend on open granite, this time to a large, sandy-bottomed pool below a spectacular cataract on Summit City Creek. This pool makes a fine lunch spot.

From the pool we pick up the ducked route again and make two half-loops away from the creek and back to it. In some places there are competing ducks, but they all lead in the correct general direction. About ¼ mile from the pool we get a good look down into the river canyon, and see that it is not too far below us now. After the second half-loop returns to the creek momentarily, our route veers east, tops a small ridge, and descends steeply south for ¼ mile to a crossing of Summit City Creek. A fallen tree here still with its bark, which does not quite reach the north bank, would help one across the

The Mokelumne River above Camp Irene

creek during high water. About 100 yards beyond the crossing, a faint trail forks left. (If you followed it 300 yards to an unsigned junction in a sandy flat, turned right, and went 300 more yards, you'd come to a sign indicating *Cedar CampTrail* close to the beautiful Mokelumne River.)

Foregoing this side trip, we turn left, top a small ridge, cross a tributary stream, and descend into a dense forest of second-growth ponderosa pine and incense-cedar with a few delicate ferns on the level forest floor. Then, emerging from this forest, we see that we are close under granite cliffs on the right (north). From here a gentle downgrade takes us past a 5-foot-thick ponderosa, burned through at the base, into a fine forest of first-growth sugar pines, their great cones strewn about the forest floor. After crossing a stream that flows in early season, our route soon leaves the forest and climbs more than 100 feet on rocky-dusty underfooting, leveling off under a sparse-to-moderate cover of Jeffrey pines, incense-cedars and black oaks. In 1/8 mile after the climb, the eastbound hiker would notice a fork veering right, but he should keep left. From this junction our path makes a steep, sandy ascent for several hundred yards, then drops slightly across exposed granite outcroppings. Just after it swings right, there is another unofficial junction that might beguile an eastbound hiker: he should keep right at this junction. Then one arrives at the signed junction of the trails to Camp Irene (left) and Munson Meadow (right).

From this junction our trail descends moderately to steeply, very soon emerging onto granite slabs where the route is marked only by ducks. Then it veers right and comes close to an all-year stream not shown on the topo map, whose merry song we have for a few minutes been hearing. Soon we re-enter forest cover of white fir, incense-cedar, black oak, and ponderosa and silver pine, and then descend for 1/3 mile near the creek in cool shade where hundreds of bracken ferns carpet the forest floor. Afterward, the trail becomes less steep and veers left out of earshot of the singing stream and down onto the forested flats of the Mokelumne River canyon. In a few hundred yards we reach the ford called Camp Irene, where the good campsites are highly used all summer. In August 1978 a down tree extended most of the way from the north bank to the south, and the remaining open water could be crossed on boulders. But in early season, or if floods have widened the area of open water, you may have to get pretty wet crossing the river. A rope properly used here can make for a safe crossing.

Beyond the ford, the trail climbs for almost a mile, sometimes moderately and sometimes steeply, under the same forest cover we saw below the trail junction on the north canyon wall. Then the trail reaches open slopes where a few black oaks dot the hillside of granite bedrock and boulders half-covered by huckleberry oak and manzanita bushes. Here also we encounter the first of a long series of blasted granite areas where it seems the Forest Service went beyond the call of duty in its use of dynamite. One result is the many rocks on the trail, which make going up difficult and going down worse. On these open slopes the trail makes eight switchbacks before touching the Underwood Valley stream, and afterwards almost touches it five more times. It then leads southwest away from the stream, switchbacks several more times and

The log crossing at Camp Irene

see MAP 7

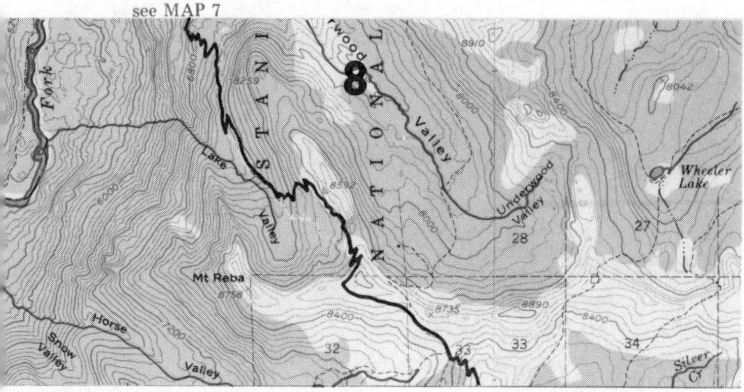

follows ducks up open granite slabs. Then you parallel the stream for 50 yards and come to a switchback overlooking the stream only 7 yards away. This is your last water for about 2 miles in mid and late season.

Beyond the drinking pool, the trail switchbacks again, overlooking a flat area beside the stream with some fair campsites. After passing below a cliff that stands southwest of us, we switchback some more and then, heading southeast, struggle

Last water at Underwood Valley stream

Lake Valley

up toward the last and highest cliff visible along this trail section. Then the route turns right and leads southwest about ¼ mile as it descends slightly to an overlook of the Mokelumne River canyon in the west, with the Mokelumne Tetons and rusty Mokelumne Peak rising grandly on the north canyon wall.

From this viewpoint we climb up a moderate grade which is bordered by thousands of wildflowers and dampened by dozens of freshets in early-to-mid season. A few more switchbacks then bring the Yosemite-bound hiker to a modest campsite right beside the trail, overlooking the first water for 2 miles (in mid and late season). In a few minutes we reach a larger, nicer campsite right beside the Lake Valley stream, the first water in several miles for northbound hikers. Climbing slightly from the campsite, our route passes just above a flat area that once was a lake and then begins a long series of switchbacks up the east wall of Lake Valley. This wall is capped by dark volcanic outcroppings from which boulders have broken off and rolled down to the trail and beyond. This is Pliocene pyroclastic ("fire-broken") rock, a dark lava matrix containing many large inclusions of older igneous rock.

Finally, at a saddle east of Mt. Reba, we leave the Mokelumne Wilderness at an elevation of 8750 feet. Now on dirt road open to motor vehicles, we stroll through what could be the world's largest field of mule ears. In early season, their large yellow flowers and very large green leaves are a chromatic wonder. In mid-to-late season, the dry leaves rattle fiercely in the stiff breezes always present here in the afternoon. At the first intersection beyond the wilderness boundary, which is unsigned, we have no indecision, but a northbound hiker must remember to take the left-hand trail. In about ¾ mile from the wilderness, your road-trail reaches a low point and forks there. One branch goes uphill south, and our branch goes uphill east 30 yards to a saddle. In this saddle a large silver pine bears black **I** blazes on both its east and its west sides.

Beyond this tree the trail goes straight downhill for about 200 yards, then veers right and traverses downslope on an exposed, steep, dusty descent for 1 mile to a jump-across all-year stream. This dry stretch is relieved by good views of volcanic towers to the east and by many flowers in mid-to-late season. The hillside has large areas of pennyroyal, which in the warm afternoon sun give off a very pleasant, pungent scent. About 400 yards beyond the all-year stream the Wheeler Lake Trail goes off to the left (northeast). Our descending trail, now well-shaded and no longer steep, reaches another junction in ¾ mile, where a trail signed *Alpine bypass* and marked by white **I** blazes on tree boles takes off to the right (southwest). Here we go straight, following a sign that indicates Highway 4 is ½ mile ahead. In just 175 yards we reach a road at an unsigned junction. Here we turn left (east) and in a few yards cross Bee Gulch, where water flows into mid season. Immediately this little road veers right, and we leave it to tread a trail marked by black **I** blazes on tree trunks. An unsigned, unmapped trail leads up the east side of Bee Gulch, but we ignore it. The black **I** blazes show the way for the last ½ mile, most of it lodgepole-shaded, to Highway 4, at a point between the entrance to Chickaree Picnic Area on the west and the road to Pine Marten and Silver Valley campgrounds on the east. The Lake Alpine Resort is 0.7 mile west on the highway.

see MAP 8

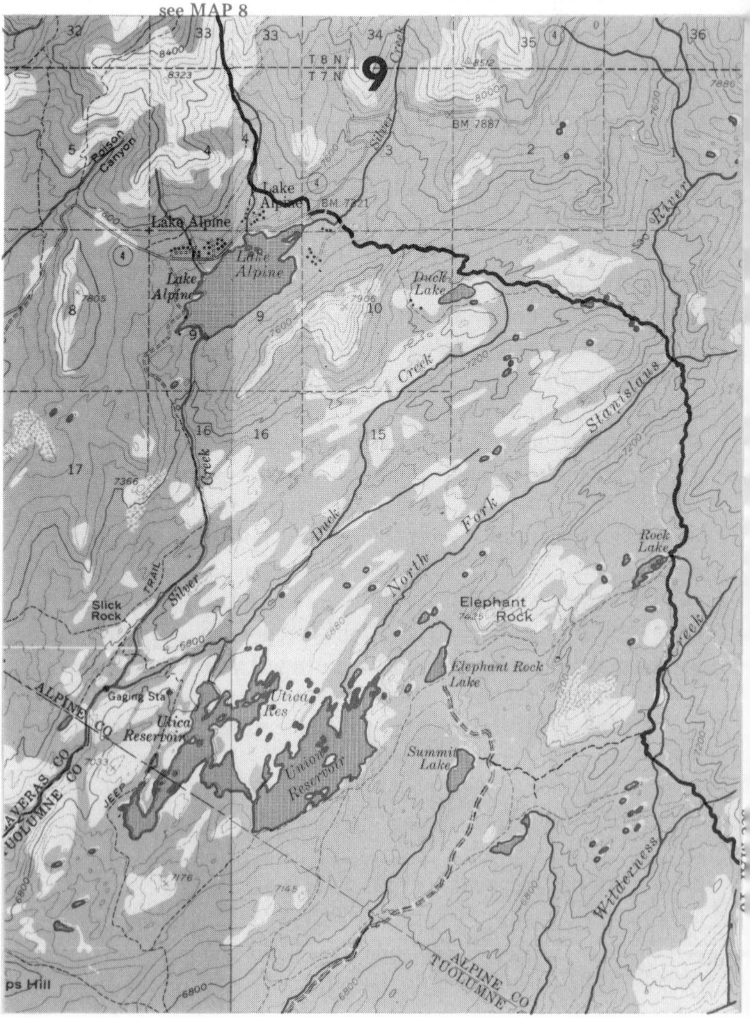
9
T 8 N
T 7 N
Poison Canyon
Lake Alpine
Lake Alpine
Lake Alpine
Lake Alpine
BM 7887
BM 7821
Silver Creek
Duck Lake
Creek
Duck
Stanislaus
North Fork
River
Rock Lake
Elephant Rock
Elephant Rock Lake
Slick Rock
TRAIL
Silver
Creek
Gaging Sta
Utica Res
Utica Reservoir
Union Reservoir
Summit Lake
ALPINE CO
CALAVERAS CO
TUOLUMNE CO
JEEP
Wilderness
Creek
ALPINE CO
TUOLUMNE CO
ps Hill

IV. LAKE ALPINE TO CLARK FORK

This section of the Tahoe-Yosemite Trail is the most timbered section, and the one with the least elevation change per mile. It provides a rest for the senses which have been almost overstimulated by the intense variety of the previous sections, and which will again be assailed by awesome majesties as we get nearer to Yosemite.

Despite the large amount of timber in this section, there are, in mid and late summer, long dry stretches, and a water bottle is mandatory.

Since not everyone who reads this book is doing the whole Tahoe-Yosemite Trail, it's worth mentioning that the first 2½ miles of this section are on underfooting that is very suitable for jogging. A run from Lake Alpine to the North Fork Stanislaus River and back is highly recommended.

Just 0.7 mile east of Lake Alpine Resort a dirt road leads south to several campgrounds. The first is for backpackers only, only 0.1 mile from the highway. Then, beyond often-dry Silver Creek, a road branch leads right to Pine Marten campground. About 150 yards later, the road veers right (west) toward Silver Valley Campground, and we spy a closed-off road signed *No vehicles* leading south between two large boulders. On this old road we ascend gently for ¼ mile through a red-fir and lodgepole forest dotted with flowering meadows to a low, timbered ridge, and then follow the ridge northeast through a stock gate. About 200 yards down the far side of the ridge, our road makes a sharp bend, and we leave it for a recently built trail segment that bypasses Duck Lake. This dusty segment descends gently to moderately under a forest cover of ponderosa pines, with some mountain junipers and white firs mixed in.

Soon the path levels, and then passes about 150 yards from the north end of Duck Lake, barely seen through the forest of lodgepole pines. Now winding through a boggy flat, we dodge hordes of mosquitoes—if it's early season—and hurry to a junction with an abandoned segment of the Highland Creek Trail. East of this fork our trail climbs gently to a low saddle overlooking the verdant canyon of the North Fork Stanislaus River. Immediately we make a gentle descent under the welcome shade of red firs, lodgepole pines and junipers, arriving in ½ mile at the Stanislaus fork. Fair campsites are plentiful on both sides of the boulder-hop ford. In early season when the water is too high to cross here, you can probably find logs about 100 yards upstream. Fill your water bottle.

Beyond the river, the Tahoe-Yosemite Trail climbs south for 400 vertical feet in two stages—a short one and then a long one—to a gently sloping ridge with undistinguished views westward. Then, via a two-stage descent of more modest proportions we arrive at the dry-in-late-summer outlet of shallow, marshy Rock Lake. There are some good campsites on the

Rock Lake

southeast shore, amid thick stands of fir and pine, and the lake is one of the warmer swimming spots along the Tahoe-Yosemite Trail.

The trail beyond the outlet of Rock Lake ascends gently for a short way and then drops almost to the banks of Wilderness Creek, where you can find potable water except in late summer and early fall of normal years. Then we veer southwest away from the stream and cross a dry, open, sandy flat on which grows much mat lupine, backgrounded by many red firs and junipers. About 1½ miles from Rock Lake we pass the Sand Flat Trail, leading west, and then descend on pleasant duff underfooting to the ford of Wilderness Creek, where there are a few fair campsites.

Beyond this crossing the Tahoe-Yosemite Trail rises gently to moderately, through the gray outcroppings dotted with Jeffrey pines, and brings us to a viewpoint from which we can look across Highland Creek canyon to the chocolate-colored, layered volcanic formations on the southern horizon called the Dardanelles. Eastward up the canyon of Highland Creek are views of Hiram, Airola and Iceberg peaks, each of them reaching above timberline to almost 10,000 feet. Beyond this viewpoint our trail is steep and exposed on its descent to Gabbot Meadow beside Highland Creek.

The descent ends at a fence in the meadow, and our trail turns left to follow the fence line for 300 yards to a gate, through which the Highland Creek Trail starts south, then quickly veers east. The Tahoe-Yosemite Trail parallels the fence for another ¼ mile to another gate, from which you can hike 250 yards southeast to campsites near Highland Creek. There are fair-to-good campsites in several parts of Gabbot Meadow, but the area is shared with a large bovine population. Yet at night the singing, howling and yipping of coyotes restore the feeling of wilderness. From the second gate we continue to parallel the fence for another ¼ mile, to where the fence ends and the trail approaches the creek.

Leaving the fence behind, we ascend gently, cross Bull Run Creek and pass the trail to Pacific Valley. The stream-sculpted granite bedrock exposed at low water along Highland Creek

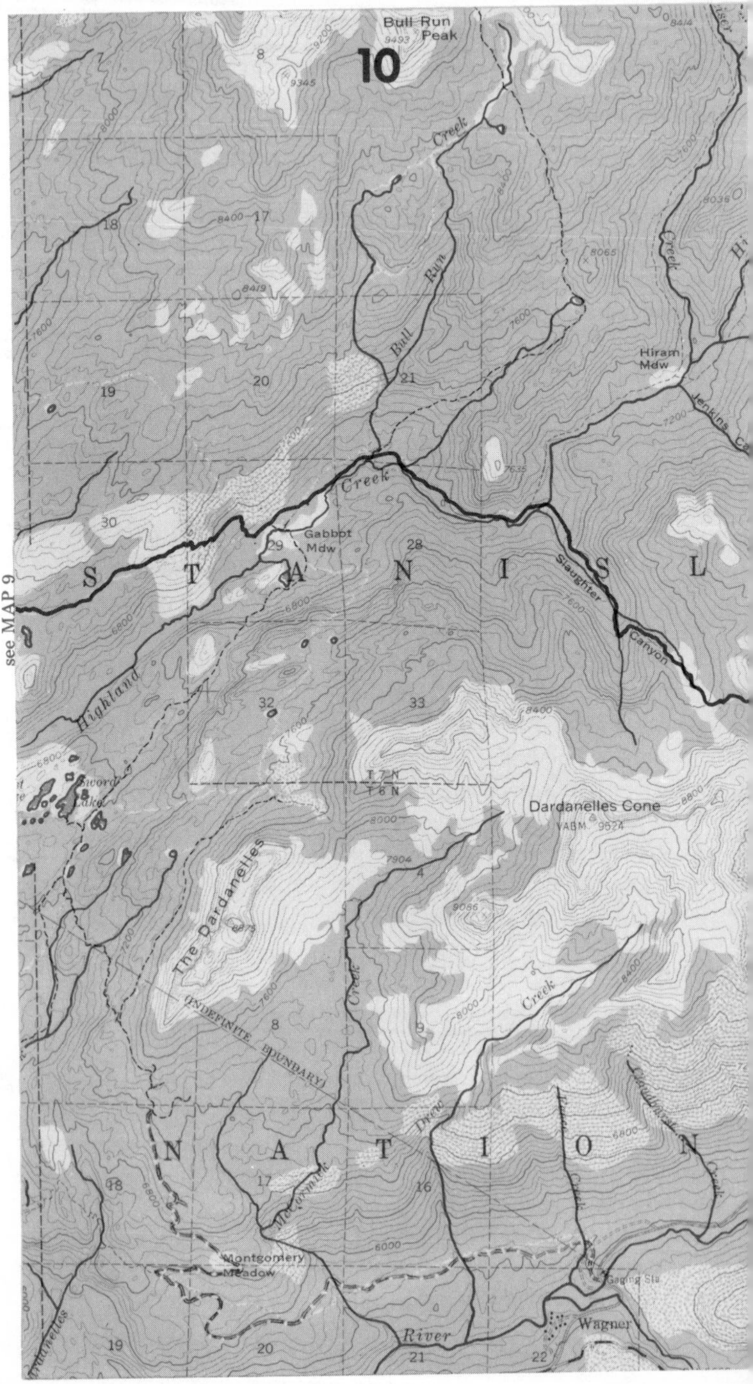
Bull Run Peak
9493
10
Creek
Bull Run
Hiram Mdw
Jenkins
Gabbot Mdw
Creek
S T A N I S L
Slaughter Canyon
Highland
Sword Lake
T 7 N
T 6 N
Dardanelles Cone
VABM 9524
The Dardanelles
INDEFINITE BOUNDARY
Creek
Creek
Drew
N A T I O N
McCormick
Montgomery Meadow
River
Wagner
Gaging Sta

see MAP 9

will claim the photographer's attention, and fly fisherman like the succulent rainbow trout that fin beneath willow branches. This gentle ascent brings us to the junction of the Highland Creek Trail with the Jenkins Canyon Trail. (Jenkins Canyon is incorrectly called Slaughter Canyon of the topo map. All the canyon labels on the topo map from "Poison Canyon" to "Slaughter Canyon" should be moved one canyon to the southwest; the canyon labeled "Poison" on the map is actually unnamed.) There is a good campsite across Highland Creek 100 yards downstream from this junction.

The Jenkins Canyon Trail, bound for Woods Gulch, arrives in 60 yards at the west bank of Highland Creek, and we cross it on boulders near its confluence with Jenkins Canyon creek. The trail resumes on the east bank just 20 yards above the confluence and climbs steeply through a heavy forest cover. Then it becomes almost level and contours along the canyon slope above the stream. On this stretch of trail we can see an unusual sight: within a few yards of one another are specimens of every tree that is found *anywhere* in this section of the Tahoe-Yosemite Trail: Jeffrey, ponderosa, silver and lodgepole pine; red and white fir; mountain juniper, aspen, and black cottonwood. Shortly after beginning another moderate ascent, we encounter broken volcanic rock lying on the ground, evidence that we are nearing the great igneous outpourings which created the Dardanelles and Dardanelles Cone. The trail crosses the east fork of Jenkins Canyon creek and then ascends steeply to a meadow which shows too much evidence of use—both erosion and litter—by grazing stock and deer hunters. The grass in this quarter-mile-long meadow is interrupted by stands of young red firs, and willows that turn flame-yellow in September.

A moderate ascent of ½ mile from the campsites takes us to the saddle that divides Jenkins Canyon from Woods Gulch. The hiker should take care to close the stock gate here—and whenever he encounters one—in order to prevent stock from overgrazing some areas while using others below their capacity. As we begin the descent into Woods Gulch, the vegetation changes markedly, with the appearance of huckleberry oak, chinquapin and sagebrush. The south-facing slope above the trail is covered with stands of sagebrush, and among these desert shrubs, a thousand mule-ear plants bear their yellow flowers in summer. Across the little valley, the north-facing slope is thoroughly shaded by red fir and lodgepole pine trees.

Beyond the saddle, the sandy trail descends moderately and then gently, crossing the unnamed streams that drain Woods Gulch. As the forest cover of red fir thickens, the descent quickens, becoming moderate and then steep. Finally we switchback 500 rocky feet down a badly eroded, dusty trail. Then our trail levels off and crosses the main stream in Woods Gulch. Beyond the ford we turn east to descend gently beside the stream under a moderate cover of white fir, incense-cedar and aspen. After less than ½ mile we meet the Arnot Creek Trail, a jeep road, and turn right (south) onto it, arriving in 100 yards at a final ford of Woods Gulch creek.

For almost 2 miles now we follow this well-used jeep road, passing many campsites used mostly by four-wheel-borne outdoorsmen. Finally reaching a gate, we find a trail that arcs southeast to a trailhead parking lot. From the lot a dirt road leads southwest to the blacktop, deadend Clark Fork Highway. There is no clear, official route for the Tahoe-Yosemite Trail in this area, so if you are a through-hiker, you might as well continue south on your own route to the highway. If you don't mind the civilization, you can camp at the Riverview Campground, beside the river near the junction of the highway with the dirt road mentioned above, or at Sand Flat.
It is 24 miles southwest to the little settlement of Strawberry on Highway 108, and 15 miles up Highway 108 to Kennedy Meadow. Some Tahoe-Yosemite trekkers hitch a ride from the end of the Arnot Creek jeep road to Kennedy Meadow and then resume hiking southward, but they not only fail to do the whole trail—they miss the beauties of the Clark Fork section.

V. CLARK FORK TO KENNEDY MEADOW

This section of the Tahoe-Yosemite Trail takes us on a long climb up a deep canyon to a large meadow in a steep-walled basin. The meadow, Clark Fork Meadow, is one of the largest along the trail. From the meadow we take a wild and high cross-country route to the highest point on the entire Tahoe-Yosemite Trail at a little saddle called St. Marys Pass.

A mile beyond the pass our route joins the Sonora Pass Highway (State Route 108) and we parallel the road for 10 downhill miles to Kennedy Meadow.

For 3.7 miles our route proceeds beside the deadend blacktop road. The construction of an actual trail beside the Clark Fork of the Stanislaus River is unfortunately of low priority in Forest Service plans, and the traveler will have to choose his own route until a trail can be built here. But as walks beside roads go, it's a nice walk, and one can spend the time contemplating why the south wall of the canyon is forested and the north is dry brush.

At Iceberg Meadow the road ends, and the Tahoe-Yosemite Trail continues eastward past a picnic ground next to the river (overnight camping prohibited). Our route ascends gently for a few hundred yards before making a short, steep climb out of the incense-cedar zone into the fir belt. From here it is 2 easy miles to the ford of Boulder Creek, our route being mostly within sight or sound of alder- and willow-lined Clark Fork. The underfooting is alternately sand and duff, and the forest cover is moderate-to-dense red and white fir and Jeffrey pine. There are several good streamside campsites along this stretch of trail, and the wet banks of the tributaries host columbine, monkey flower and other moisture-loving flowers.

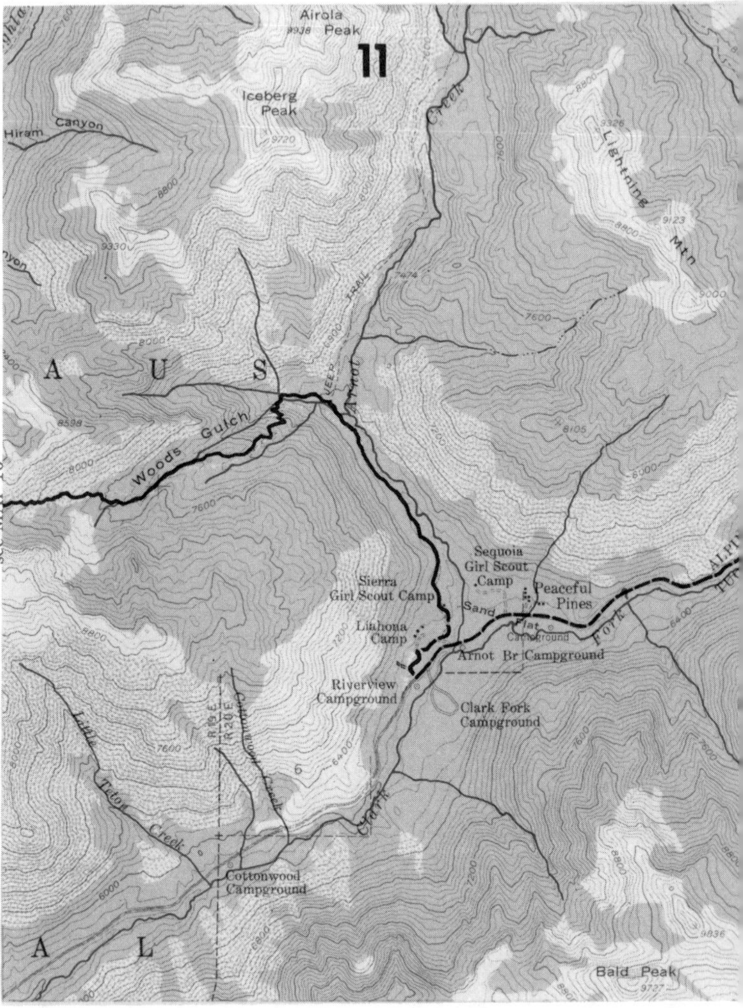

see MAP 10

Just before the crossing of Boulder Creek an unsigned trail departs up the creek's canyon. This side trail looks to be more used than the main one, and many hikers have mistakenly gone some distance up it. But the Tahoe-Yosemite Trail veers right (south) and ascends more and more steeply, climbing toward

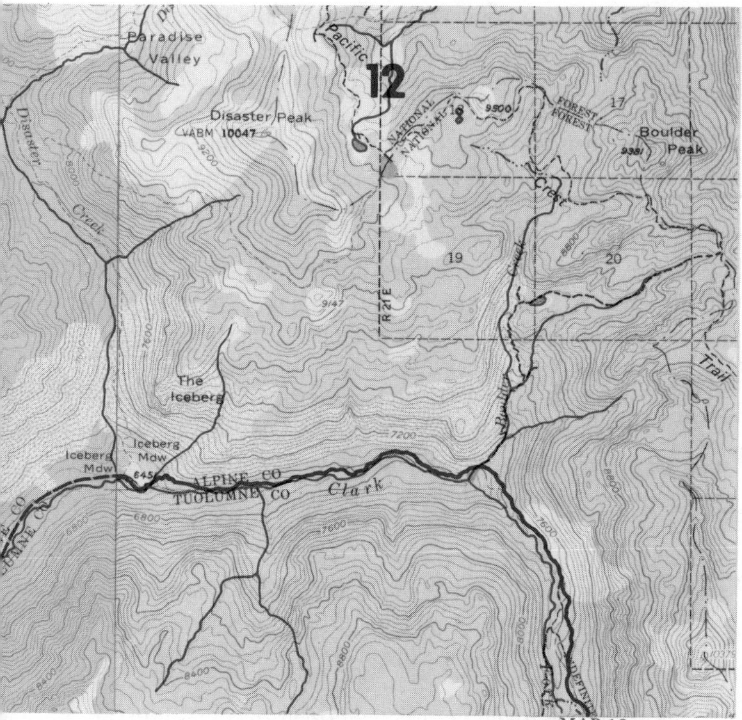

see MAP 13

the highest point on the entire trail, at St. Marys Pass. Soon the grade becomes very steep, on rocky-dusty underfooting beside the cascading Clark Fork. The northbound hiker's first views of the spectacular Dardanelles are to be had from this trail section. Where the climb levels off, we come to a trail fork and take the right-hand branch.

Beyond the top of the climb, the trail passes a meadow on the stream boasting aspen, alder, willow, lodgepole, black cottonwood, fair campsites, and a nighttime complement of foraging mammals. About 1/3 mile beyond this meadow is a prominent **Y** fork in the trail. Either fork will lead to the same place in less than a mile, and both forks have some indistinct sections before they rejoin. Cows graze all over this slope, and some of the "trails" are merely cowpaths.

Beyond these sloping meadows the sandy trail veers east up an exposed, sage-dotted slope to ford a stream, and then it continues its ascent under a moderate forest cover of white and red fir, juniper, and lodgepole and silver pine. Although the topo map shows no tributary streams in this section of trail, there is one about every ½ mile, draining the granite ridge that forms the Sierra crest here. This long, gentle ascent finally brings us to a boulder ford of the Clark Fork beside several fair-to-good campsites. Just before these camps a trail branches left, but our route continues fairly straight. After the ford, the ascent increases to moderate and then steep, winding among hemlocks, silver pines, and lodgepoles, and leaving red firs behind. From here our route is ducked over large granite outcroppings to the foot of Clark Fork Meadow, a very large, open grassland almost encircled by steep walls of pine-and-hemlock-dotted granite. Above the granite this upper basin is rimmed by reddish-brown and tan volcanic rocks, which are bare of trees except for a few clumps of whitebark pine. There are numerous good campsites around the meadow, and a superb display of mountain flowers in season. It is hard to imagine that there is a state highway just over the ridge to the south.

Hikers have found or invented dozens of routes into (northbound) or out of (southbound) Clark Fork Meadow, and the one I describe is not the only safe one, but I believe it is the easiest to follow, and the easiest to hike.

Beyond the head of the meadow, we continue in forest on a trail of sorts near the stream. Then, a few hundred feet after we cross a northeast-bank tributary, we come to a split in the stream. Here we cross the east fork on a log and turn directly uphill beside the other fork, close under a granite cliff to the east of our route. For the first ½ mile the occasionally ducked ascent is quite steep, but it is mercifully shadded by moderate-to-dense hemlock forest.

Where the slope decreases and the tree cover thins, we begin to veer east. This route takes us onto a ridge dotted with whitebark pines, and we stroll across volcanic rock and granite at timberline, where the gravelly soil is a garden of wildflowers

see MAP 12

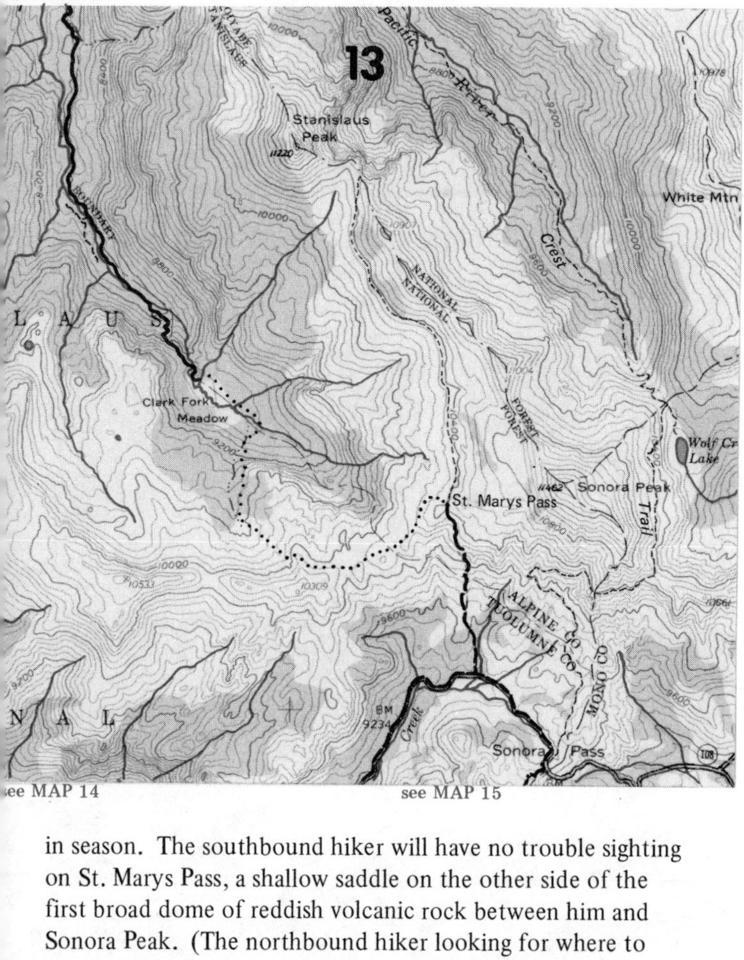

see MAP 14

see MAP 15

in season. The southbound hiker will have no trouble sighting on St. Marys Pass, a shallow saddle on the other side of the first broad dome of reddish volcanic rock between him and Sonora Peak. (The northbound hiker looking for where to begin his major descent into the meadow should begin to veer north as soon as he has passed beyond the billowy granite outcroppings that line most of the route for the first mile or so from St. Marys Pass. Here begins the little stream that flows down past the symbol "9200" on the topo map, and the northbound route follows the ridge that lies northeast of this stream's upper drainage basin, then at about timberline drops down to parallel the stream.)

The trail south from St. Marys Pass is easy to follow, as it soon leads to a jeep road (shown as a trail on the topo map) which covers the last mile to Sonora Pass Highway. This dirt road meets the Sonora Pass Highway (108) 1 mile west of the pass. From here you could avoid losing 3100 feet of altitude by walking the l mile to Sonora Pass and following the Pacific Crest Trail south 8.1 miles to meet a closed jeep road at a switchback, then following the road south 7.8 miles to Grizzly Meadows to remeet the Tahoe-Yosemite Trail.

Our route turns west beside the blacktop road and begins what is the longest roadside stretch of the Tahoe-Yosemite Trail. The sparsely timbered high valley here is dominated by the jagged crest of rich, dark volcanic rock on the south. Three of the snowfields you can see high under the ridge ahead are little glaciers.

Soon the road makes a steep ascent to penetrate the 9000-foot contour, then turns sharply right into the charming vale called Chipmunk Flat. There are good campsites near Deadman Creek at several places in this high valley. At the lower end of Chipmunk Flat is a Historical Site sign, pointing out the old grade of the Sonora/Mono Toll Road. Early immigrants

Looking south from St. Marys Pass

crossing the Sierra in this area came over Emigrant Pass, but with the discovery of gold in Aurora, on the east side of the Sierra, demand rose for a better route. Surveys for a road over Sonora Pass were made in 1860-63, and after a Clark Fork/St. Marys Pass route was rejected, the road was completed in 1865. Over the years, various realignments finally resulted in a completed surfaced Sonora Pass road in the early 1940s.

The walk down this canyon provides an excellent opportunity for the amateur dendrologist to observe the different tree belts. Starting with whitebark pine near St. Marys Pass and lodgepole pine near Sonora Pass, the descent encounters silver pine (where Blue Canyon Creek enters), red fir (at Chipmunk Flat), mountain juniper, Jeffrey pine, incense-cedar and canyon live oak (around 7500′), white fir (above 7000′), and sugar pine (at about 6800′, which is near the upper limit of its range). Finally, at the foot of the long, long descent, we see the first broadleaf deciduous tree (excepting aspen)–black oak.

Beyond Chipmunk Flat the road rises moderately as the creek descends, and soon we are far above the cascading water. From a level stretch of road, we can look across the canyon of the Middle Fork Stanislaus River to peaks nearly 10,000 feet in elevation. The road then descends gently under a sparse forest cover of young firs and Jeffrey pines, with a ground cover largely composed of manzanita, plus some sagebrush. Where the road makes a switchback and turns sharply left, there are excellent views up the canyon of the Stanislaus to Granite Dome, which seems to stand athwart the canyon almost like a gigantic dam.

Over 9 miles from where we began this roadside walk, we turn left on a paved road that rises gently for 1 mile to Kennedy Meadow resort. At the far end of the resort is a parking lot, where we will thankfully resume trail walking. The hiker who would prefer to avoid the population explosion around Kennedy Meadow should plan to camp in Chipmunk Flat, so that on the next day he can without too much effort get into wilderness again.

VI. KENNEDY MEADOW TO TUOLUMNE MEADOWS

The 71-mile finale of the Tahoe-Yosemite Trail takes the hiker through the Emigrant Wilderness and over Bond Pass into Yosemite's famous north boundary country. This is the longest length of the trail uncrossed by a highway, and it passes through the largest roadless area in California. Ahead lie the grand pleasures of a backcountry walk.

The long ascent through Emigrant Basin takes us from the densely forested canyons of Summit Creek to the panoramic vistas of Emigrant Meadow. After crossing the border into Yosemite, our trail will lead across canyons that were carved by mighty glaciers, through lush meadows that were once lakes, and past other lakes that are still mountain jewels. This section of the trail is a preview of the true High Sierra on the other side of our destination, Tuolumne Meadows.

(If you are doing just this part of the Tahoe-Yosemite Trail, you can park a car free on the side road to Kennedy Meadow resort anywhere north of the bridge just before you reach the resort, or for a fee in the resort's parking area.) This resort is the main gateway to the Emigrant Wilderness. You can rent horses and mules, buy restaurant meals, sleep in wooden cabins or camp out—for a fee. You can also buy food in the grocery store, but the choice is small and the style is not backpacking style.

From a gate beside the Middle Fork Stanislaus River, our route follows an old dirt road over a small ridge to Kennedy Meadow proper and skirts the east side of the large meadow. From this road you have sweeping views of the winding river and lush grasslands, and at the north end you may spy some wooden construction that looks "old West" but is in fact the remains of a movie set ("Mail-Order Bride"). Beyond the meadow, the trail crosses the river via a bridge and immediately veers west onto a trail section constructed in 1969 after a record snowmelt washed out a bridge on the section it replaces.

This trail section ascends gently past the foot of a small granite dome and then switchbacks up a steeper grade between this dome and its larger neighbor. Under a sparse-to-moderate forest cover of mixed conifers, the route ascends steadily up a little canyon to a saddle, where it turns eastward to descend a sandy, multi-tracked slope to Summit Creek, entering the 106,910-acre Emigrant Wilderness. After paralleling the creek for a few steps, the trail crosses it on a bridge and meets the old, abandoned trail a few yards south of the Kennedy Lake Trail junction, near a PG&E maintenance station.

Our route then contours high above the east side of Relief Reservoir. This trail paralleling the shore offers excellent views to the south and west before it descends to the timbered shallow at the Grouse Creek ford. All the campsites here show heavy use. Still, it's a treat to sit in camp in the evening with the breeze quaking the aspen leaves, and yet neither hear the wind–because you are close by a little waterfall–nor feel the wind–because you are protected by the aspens, white firs and Jeffrey pines.

From Grouse Creek our trail undulates through mixed sparse-to-open forest, with some very large Jeffrey pines. Soon we ascend a drainage where aspen trees mark the watercourses and their fluttering leaves impart a fresh, light feeling if you pass here in the morning. Past the junction with the Lower Relief Valley Trail, our trail leaves the shaded riparian zone and enters brush-covered volcanic rubble above Summit Creek, ascending steeply on flower-bordered switchbacks. Along the rock-strewn trail here you can compare varieties of penstemon flowers in various hues.

The ascent is relieved when the trail drops into the little pocket encompassing what the map calls "Saucer Meadow," which is no longer meadow but which is campable–just barely. The gravesite indicated on the map was that of a passing immigrant, but all that remains of this last resting place is a small, vandalized sign on a tree.

see MAP 13

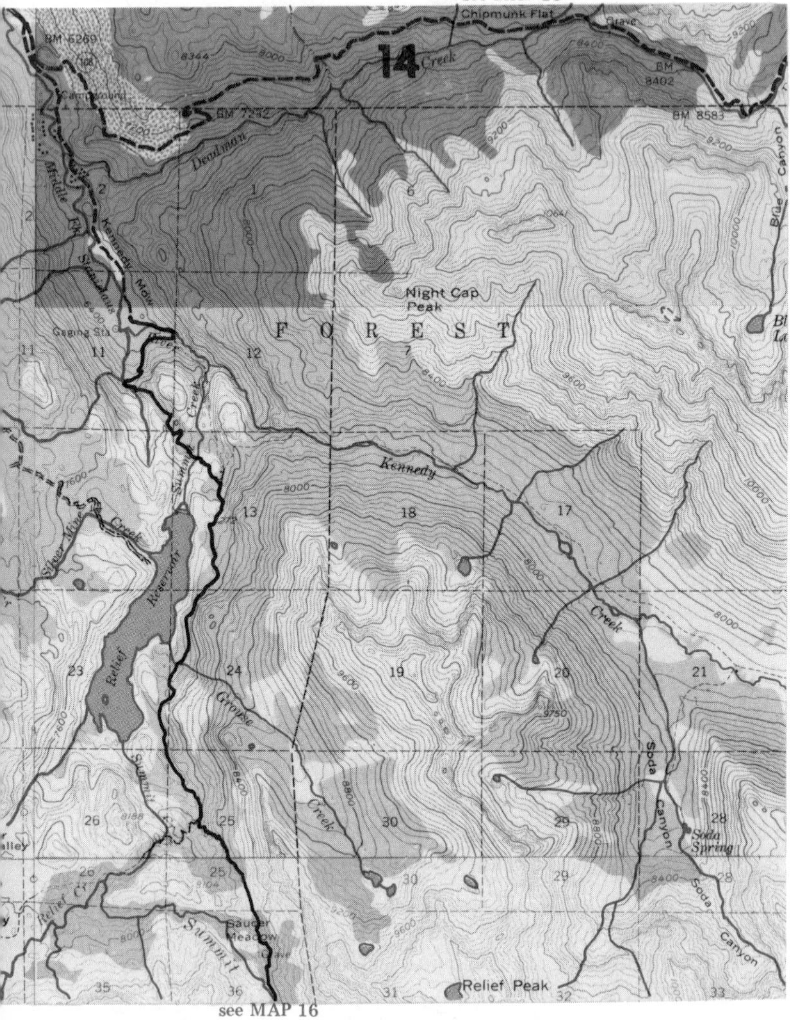

see MAP 15

see MAP 16

The section of trail beyond Saucer Meadow was once part of a major trans-Sierra route, used during the middle of the 19th century—the Emigrant Trail. With the many-hued volcanic rock of Relief Peak on the left and white, glaciated granite on the right, our trail soon reaches the alder-lined

see MAP 13

see MAP 14

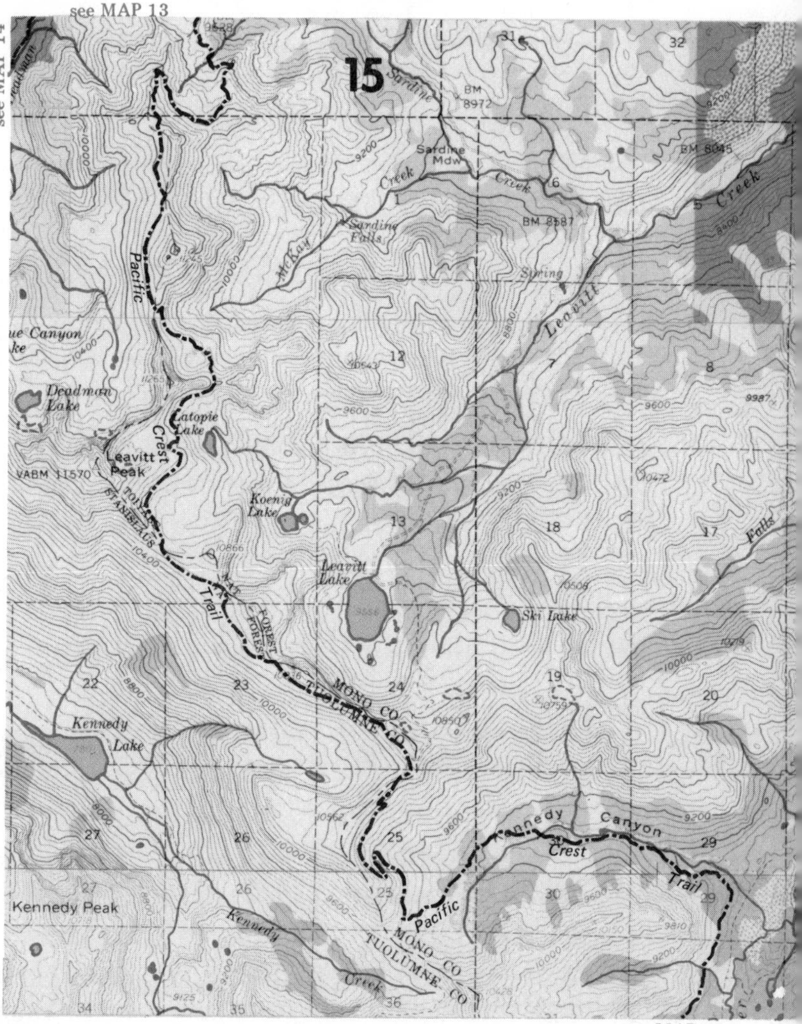

see MAP 17

banks of Summit Creek, in a little canyon full of firs, pines and junipers, where there is a wide choice of campsites. Our level trail continues up-canyon on red-fir-dotted slopes for a mile, then makes a rocky 400-foot ascent away from the creek to a little saddle which is the portal to the camping area called

Sheep Camp, another attractive and overused camping area.

By this time we have gained 2400 feet of elevation since Kennedy Meadow, and the changing tree species confirm it: red fir has dropped out and mountain hemlock has appeared. From Sheep Camp the Tahoe-Yosemite Trail ascends gently through mixed forest, broken occasionally by small fields of sagebrush. If the geology of Summit Creek canyon wasn't evident before, the sparseness of the trees here makes it easy to observe. The slopes on the left are volcanic, while those on the right are granitic. This geologic boundary can be seen all the way from Relief Reservoir to Brown Bear Pass and beyond. North of our trail above Lunch Meadow, red and black volcanic columns thrust up from the otherwise smooth, red, pumice slopes, and punctuate the skyline with their tortured shapes. South of our trail, rounded granite shapes, much more common in the Sierra, prevail.

Beyond the east end of bilobed Lunch Meadow, we ascend to meet the Emigrant Lake trail, departing south. You could camp near the creek near this junction. Then your journey becomes a steady slog, and views improve as you approach

Looking east from Brown Bear Pass

Grizzly Peak

Brown Bear Pass. It is easy to see why emigrants who used this same route relied on the distinctive outline of Relief Peak, northwest of us, as a landmark. Finally, we complete the almost unrelieved 3300-foot ascent from Kennedy Meadow and arrive at Brown Bear Pass (9700′). In the east, the grassy expanses of historic Emigrant Meadow present themselves, and the serenity of this pioneer waystop is enhanced by the placid blue waters of Emigrant Meadow Lake.

Brown Bear Pass marks the divide between the Stanislaus watershed, to the north and west, and the Tuolumne watershed, to the south and east. But this point is more than the divide between two watersheds. It is the boundary between the heavily used Summit Creek region and the more remote

see MAP 14

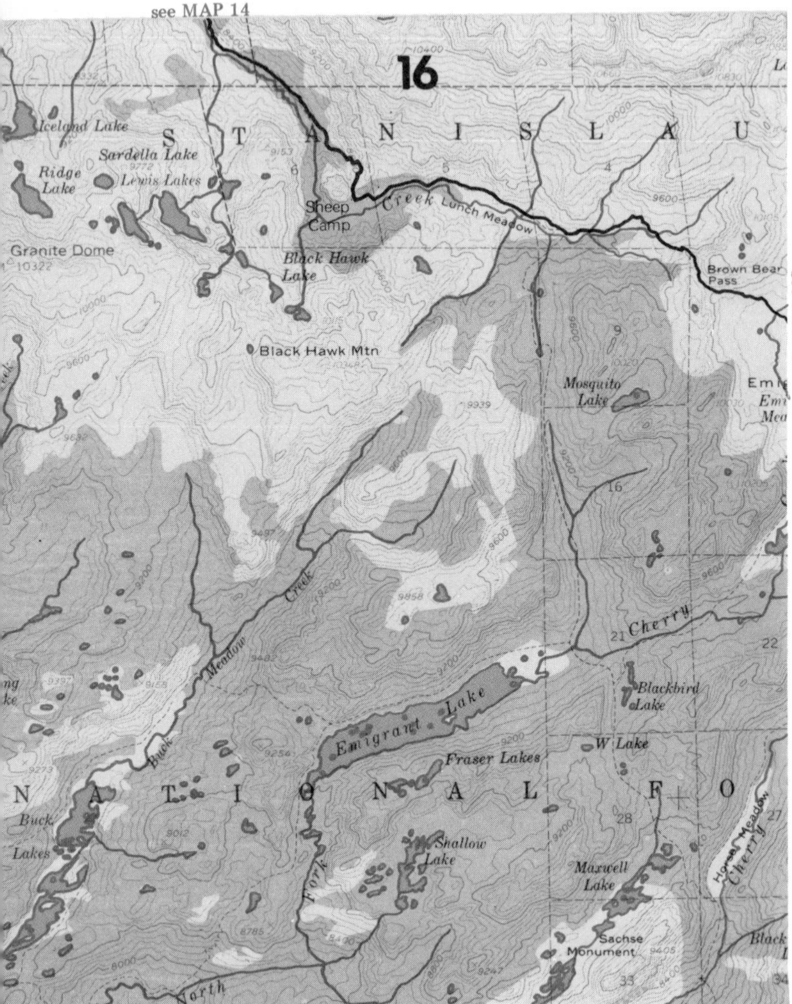

see MAP 17

and wild "north boundary country" ahead. As the trail descends from the pass on a long traverse, the visitor can't help being impressed by the gigantic scale of this grassy, granite-walled basin. It seems a fitting stage for the enactment of the "great move westward," and it doesn't take a great deal

see MAP 15

see MAP 16

see MAP 18

of imagination to hear boisterous shouts, the creaking of wagons, the barking of dogs, and the tired, hungry lowing of trail-weary stock. This great meadow saw the frenzied summertime travel of thousands of pioneers headed for the western slope, but of their passing all that remains is an echo in the wind.

Levelling off, our trail crosses the north side of Emigrant Meadow. Campsites at the lake here are rocky, windy and woodless, but fishing can be good, especially along the southwest shore. Just east of the lake, a trail leads left (north) toward High Emigrant Lake, and another leads south bound for Middle Emigrant and Emigrant lakes. Our route southeast from the junction climbs over a rocky ridge to Grizzly Meadow, with its two unnamed lakes. This area is subject to the Forest Service's Multiple-use land program; hence the traveler may encounter summer-grazing steers. Further evidences of this program mar the serenity of this backcountry ¼ mile beyond the second unnamed lake, where our trail encounters a mining road. When the Emigrant Basin Primitive Area was reclassified as the Emigrant Wilderness, some additions to it and some deletions from it were made. The one significant deletion was a corridor on both sides of this mining road from Leavitt Lake, extending right to the border of Yosemite on the east, and to within 1½ miles of Huckleberry Lake on the south. This road is open to people with mining claims who say they are seeking tungsten ore at Snow Lake and in Horse Meadow, but I view the whole thing with a very jaundiced eye. I have seen cars full of vacationing adults and children on this road on hoilday weekends, and friends have told me that hunters drive to the Yosemite border to lie in wait for Park animals that may wander over the line. Obviously, not everyone who gets past the gate on this road near Leavitt Lake is on mining business. This road-corridor is a dagger into the heart of the largest roadless area in California.

About 100 yards before we reach the road, a trail departs to the right bound for a branch of the road that runs along the East Fork Cherry Creek. A few feet down the main road a trail departs southeast along the slopes of Grizzly Peak, to remeet the Tahoe-Yosemite Trail just east of Bond Pass. Our route is the road going south, and we stroll along for a mile with good views down the valley of the East Fork Cherry Creek. Then the mining road forks, the right fork leading down the creek to several mining claims. We go straight ahead, southeast, and in a short half mile meet one more road fork.

To the right is Snow Lake and its mining "claim"; we turn left and ascend 300 feet up a moderate slope dotted with lodgepole and hemlock trees. Just before Bond Pass, at an unsigned junction, we leave the abominable road and step onto trail again, southbound. Signs at the low saddle forming the pass indicate *Yosemite National Park Boundary*, the elevation (9800′) and caution . . . *Dogs, Guns, Hunting Prohibited on Park Trails . . . Park Fire Permits required. . . .*

About ¼ mile into the Park, the high trail from the slopes of Grizzly Peak re-meets our route, and in another ¼ mile, in the midst of a descent, we reach a junction with the trail to Dorothy Lake. This trail goes straight ahead, and our Tahoe-Yosemite Trail turns right, down Jack Main Canyon.

A whole spectrum of wildlife may be found along the trail ahead, and the abundance of the wildlife is testimony to the effectiveness of the National Park system. If one is on the trail early enough, deer still out grazing will keep him entranced with their graceful movements. Ample signs of the black bears that roam this part of the Park will be found along the trail, particularly during gooseberry season. Scenically, this stretch of trail is an idyllic series of tiny meadows alongside murmuring Falls Creek. To the east, somber Forsyth Peak and

Grace Meadow

Jeff Schaffer

see MAP 17

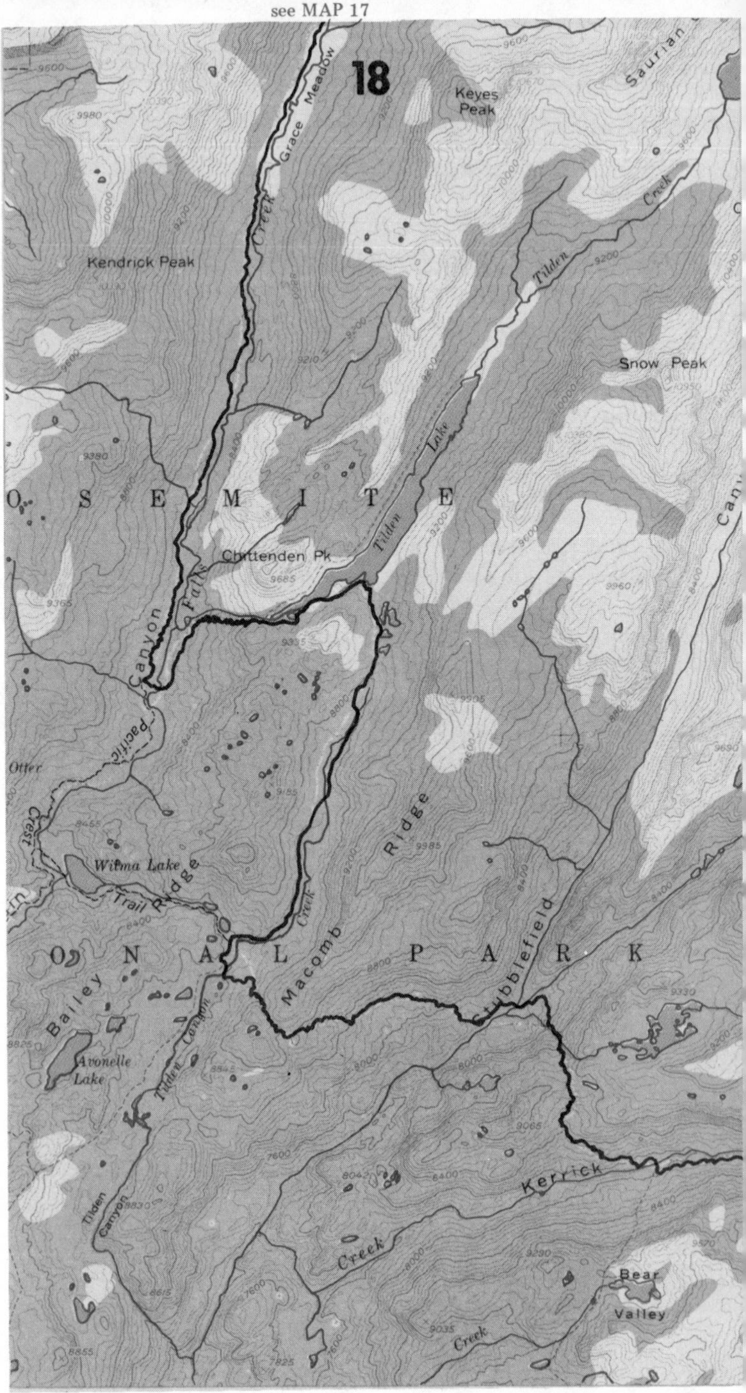
18
Grace Meadow
Creek
Keyes Peak
Saurian
Kendrick Peak
Tilden
Creek
Snow Peak
Lake
Tilden
Chittenden Pk
Falls
Canyon
O S E M I T E
Pacific
Otter
Crest
Wilma Lake
Trail
Ridge
Macomb
Ridge
Creek
Stubblefield
Canyon
O N A L P A R K
Bailey
Avonelle Lake
Tilden Canyon
Tilden Canyon
Kerrick
Creek
Bear Valley
Creek

abruptly divided Keyes Peak (juxtaposed black gabbro and white granite) cap the canyon walls. In this setting the trail gradually descends through a dense forest cover to the north end of long, rolling Grace Meadow. In contrast to wide-open, windy Emigrant Meadow, Grace Meadow has a soft, intimate feel that makes it a favorite base camp. There's good fishing for brook and rainbow trout in Falls Creek, which meanders back and forth past many potential campsites.

For the next 5 mile the trail is nearly level as it passes through numerous meadows. Much of the pathway is lined with huckleberries, and during early summer lavender shooting stars bloom in abundance along parts of the route. Chittenden Peak and its northern satellite serve as impressive reference points as we gauge our progress toward the junction where we will turn east to Tilden Lake. The sound of cascading Tilden Creek increases in volume and then it decreases, for the junction is beyond the confluence of Tilden and Falls creeks.

At this fork you turn east, cross Falls Creek in 80 yards near a good campsite, parallel the creek for ½ mile, then start to climb in earnest. Close under the steep, black-streaked south face of Chittenden Peak, the trail resolves into switchbacks so as to gain a total of more than 700 vertical feet from

Tilden Lake *National Park Service*

Falls Creek. On this rough climb you are often near crashing Tilden Creek, but not close enough for an easy drink.

Many campsites line the southeast and southwest shores of long, linear Tilden Lake, and they are well-used. At a very well-developed campsite with great views up-canyon of Saurian Crest, the trail turns south to descend through a large meadow and past a number of small tarns. Then the alternately sandy and dusty trail descends through a moderate forest cover containing small, lupine-filled meadows. Three miles from Tilden Lake the Tahoe-Yosemite Trail rejoins the Pacific Crest Trail, which it will follow to Tuolumne Meadows. The junction is 85 yards west of Tilden Canyon creek, from where the Pacific Crest Trail leads west to Wilmer Lake and then up Jack Main Canyon. A few minutes beyond, our path turns east while another goes southwest down Tilden Canyon. Beyond the boulder ford of Tilden Canyon creek we begin our traverse of the northern Yosemite "washboard." We are travelling east, and all the canyons run more or less north-south, so we have to ascend-descend-ascend until the mind reels and the feet ache. Even so, the magnificent scenery of northern Yosemite is adequate recompense for all your effort.

Your very first washboard climb has a surprise at the top that tells you you'll just have to be prepared to take what nature offers: after you have labored to top Macomb Ridge, you happily descend ¼ mile to a meadow, only to find that you have one more short, steep ascent before you begin the main descent. On this long downslope the route leaves timber to contour through low chaparral on a mountainside, then drops down a rocky, steep, cobblestoned trail to the floor of Stubblefield Canyon.

Just ¼ mile up the canyon, beside the stream, is a large camping area on the north bank and another, better one on the south, under immense red firs. After fording the creek here (difficult in early season), you are soon on switchbacks again—short, steep ones for surmounting the ridge between Stubblefield and Kerrick canyons. Halfway up, a spring flowing out of a hillside provides cool refreshment. Just beyond the shallow gap at the top is an unnamed lakelet with a generally bear-free campsite at its west end. From here the more exposed trail descends over rocky terrain past clumps of aspen and solitary junipers.

More than a mile from the lakelet you reach the floor of Kerrick Canyon and soon come to some well-developed, well-used campsites. Just beyond is the ford of Rancheria Creek on boulders (difficult in early season), and across it, a junction with the Bear Valley Trail, leading right. Now the Tahoe-Yosemite Trail begins a winding, undulating, often-ascending traverse of the south wall of Kerrick Canyon. As it passes below the heavily fractured north facade of Piute Mountain, it is sometimes high above the creek and sometimes on the creek's banks. Many tributaries, varying in size from step-across to jump-across fords, break this route segment into lush gardens of monkey flower, tiger lily, shooting star, bush lupine, corn lily, columbine and goldenrod.

At the Buckeye Pass Trail junction our route turns southwest and climbs steeply through three meretricious gaps before reaching actual Seavey Pass (9150′), 30 feet less high than the second gap before it.

From the glacially polished granite setting of Seavey Pass the trail drops past another stately rockbound tarn just below the pass, and finally plummets down over steep, eroded pitches alongside a riotous unnamed stream that feeds the Benson Lake alluvial fan. This descent is rocky going, requiring a "grunt and bear it" attitude of the downhill-weary traveler, alleviated only by the fine views of Volunteer Peak across Piute Creek and of the splashing waterfall springing from the ridge of Piute Mountain.

Where the trail levels out on the valley floor, it crosses the sandy alluvial sediments, and witnesses some drastic changes in the flora. The initial contact with the valley floor, with its solitary-standing specimens of Jeffrey pine towering amid gooseberry, gives the traveler the impression of sandy aridity. But within a few yards, the atmosphere changes as the trail becomes immersed in bracken fern, overflow freshets and dense forest. The trail is sometimes difficult to follow because of the rank growth and quagmire conditions of the valley floor.

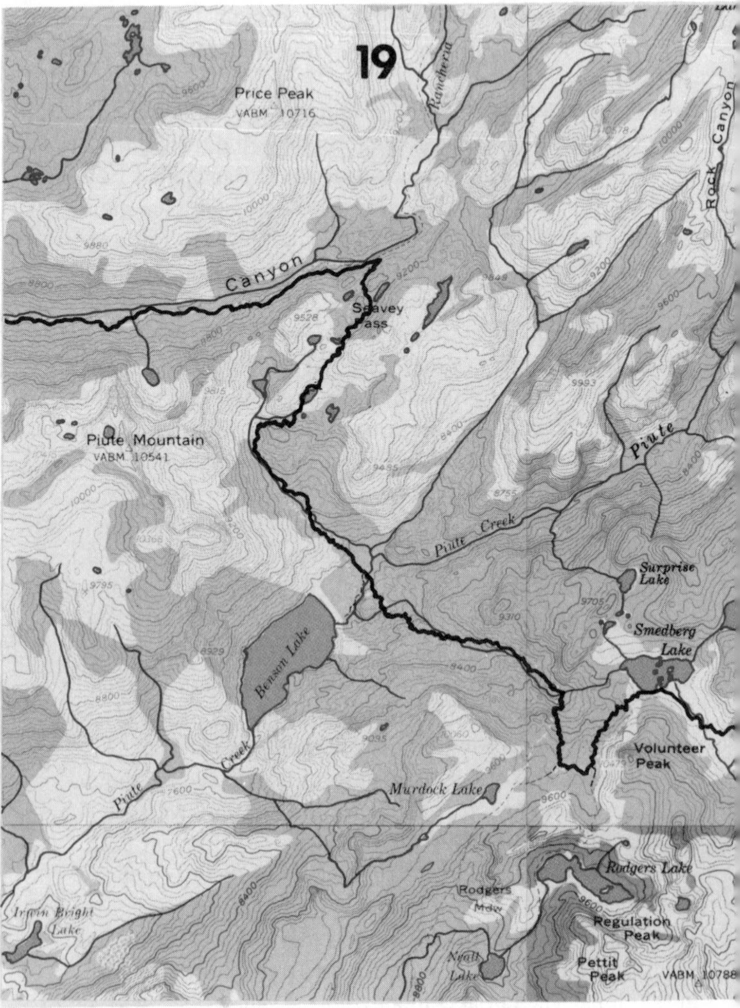

Although Benson Lake is not exactly on the Tahoe-Yosemite Trail, hardly any through-travelers fail to visit it, and neither should you. Two trails cut through this verdant area to Benson Lake. One, unmarked, turns right just after you enter the valley floor. The other departs just before the ford of Piute Creek. This lateral winds along the northwest bank of Piute Creek through fields of corn lily and bracken fern, with occasional clumps of tiger lily and swamp onion, to the good campsites along the east shore of the lake. Fishermen can look forward to good fishing for rainbow and eastern brook trout. Except in mosquito season, this lake makes a fine spot for a layover day.

Retracing our steps over the 0.3-mile lateral to the main trail, we cross Piute Creek on logs and start another of our "patented" ascents, gaining 1900 feet in 3 miles. First we climb under giant firs to a brushy saddle, then descend for 1/3 mile to a ford of Smedberg Lake's outlet creek (difficult in early season). Then we wind and switchback over metamorphic rock to another stream crossing, not as difficult. From here a steady, 1-mile moderate ascent reaches the simplest ford of this stream, and then our trail switchbacks south up to

Benson Lake

National Park Service

a junction with the Murdock Lake Trail. Just ¼ mile farther is the trail to Rodgers Lake, where you could find better camping than at crowded Smedberg Lake by walking for ½ hour out of your way.

Continuing north around the shoulder of Volunteer Peak, our trail plunges down a narrow canyon, climbs up to a ridge, and then descends to the south shore of lovely Smedberg Lake. From the narrow valley holding Smedberg Lake, the trail makes a steady climb to Benson Pass. It first follows up an inlet of Smedberg Lake on a southeast, meadowed course, then swings east on a stepladdering climb through moderate, then sparse, forest cover to an upper meadow above the main drainage feeding Smedberg Lake. After this brief respite the trail resumes its steep, rocky, upward course to Benson Pass (10,139′). The last climb is over a heavily eroded surface through sparse whitebark pine and hemlock. Excellent views to the northeast present themselves at the pass, and on the eastern flanks of the pass, weathered and blanched whitebark

Smedberg Lake *Jeff Schaffer*

pines grow directly out of the ochre scree in tight clusters about 25-50 feet apart.

Our trail from Benson Pass drops steeply, then gently, then steeply again to splashing Wilson Creek, crosses this stream, and winds down through an increasingly dense forest cover of mostly lodgepole pines. After the third ford of Wilson Creek, we plunge steeply 500 feet down through lodgepole and hemlock to the floor of deep Matterhorn Canyon. Matterhorn Canyon creek is a meandering stream flowing alternately through willowed meadows and stands of lodgepole mixed with silver pine. Our trail turns south and follows the stream a mile, to several campsites on the west bank. These canyon campsites boast several fine swimming holes just upstream in granite potholes. Fishing for eastern brook and rainbow trout is good.

Beyond the ford here (difficult in early season), we hike 80 yards northeast to a junction with the Matterhorn Canyon Trail, and turn south up the imposing, steep, forested canyon wall. About two dozen steep switchbacks help the panting trekker gain 1100 vertical feet of precious elevation, to reach a saddle where a well-earned rest will afford a chance to identify the great peaks in the north. On the left of gaping Matterhorn Canyon are Doghead and Quarry peaks and, farther away, some of the peaks of the famous Sawtooth Ridge. The great white hulk just to the right of the canyon is multi-summited Whorl Mountain, and to its right we can see the dark gray Twin Peaks ridge, pointed, rusty Virginia Peak, and pointed, light-gray Stanton Peak.

From this spectacular overlook the Tahoe-Yosemite Trail descends gently south for more than ½ mile to the meadow just north of Miller Lake, which is hemmed in by white granite walls on the east and bordered by numerous good campsites on the meadowy west side. At Miller Lake your route makes a hairpin turn and strikes out northeast on a gentle ascent past several handsome ponds. Beyond two gaps on this ascent we drop slightly to a meadowed bench, and then we rise slowly up a narrow canyon on deep gruss to a forested pass. This sodded cleft in the granite rock was the original route between

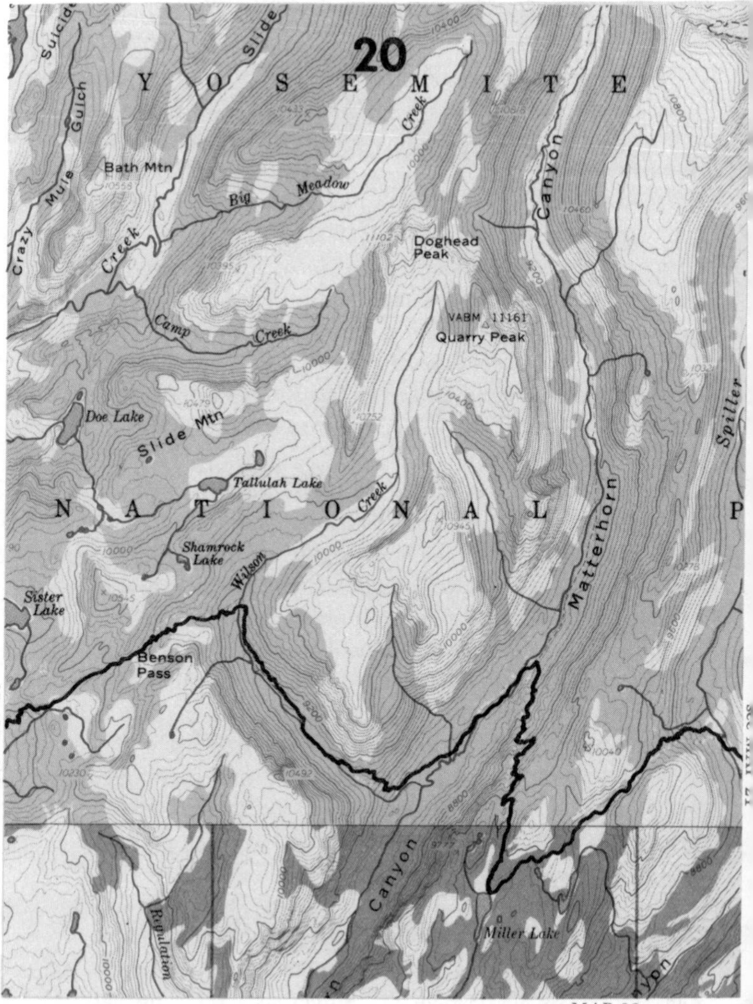

see MAP 19

see MAP 22

Spiller and Matterhorn canyons discovered by Lt. Nathaniel McClure of the 4th U.S. Cavalry in 1894, during the time that the Cavalry were the guardians of the new national park.

Now the route descends on 24 switchbacks through a moderate-to-dense forest of lodgepole and silver pine, moun-

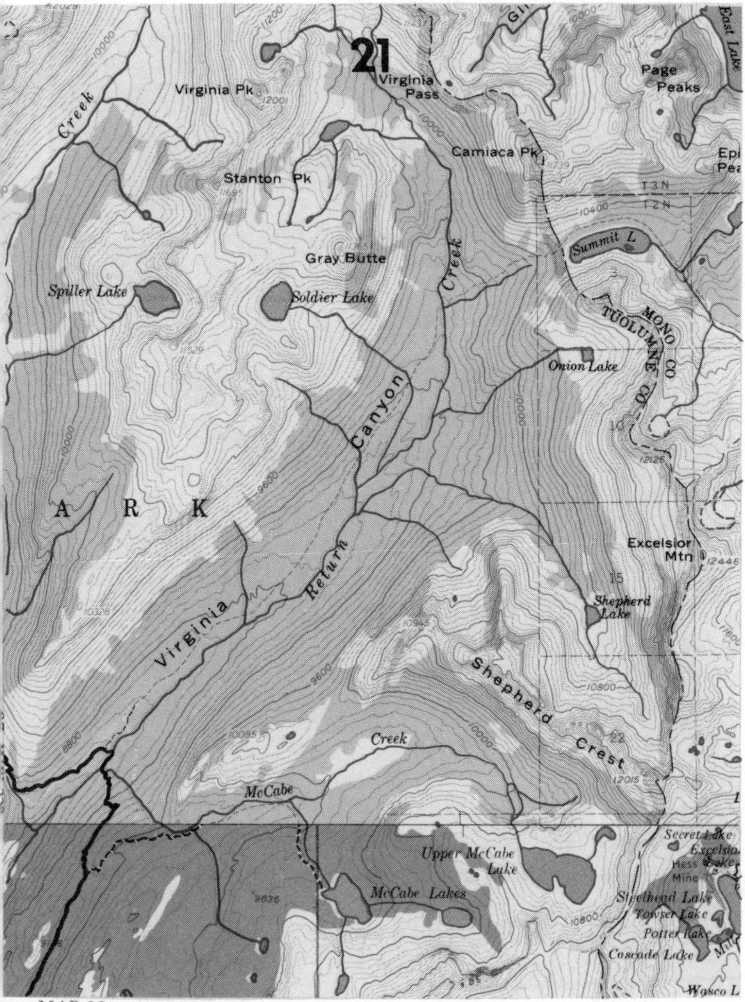

see MAP 22

tain hemlock and red fir, which give blessed shade to the northbound hiker on this steep slope. Fine views of Shepherd Crest and the Mt. Conness complex of peaks may be had through the tree breaks on this steady descent. Just beyond the boulder-hop ford on Spiller Creek (campsites nearby), an

Looking up Spiller Canyon

unmarked trail starts up Spiller Canyon. Then our rock-lined route, not far above the cascading, splashing creek, traverses southeast to round the nose of the ridge that separates Spiller and Virginia canyons, as we perhaps reflect that the "northern Yosemite washboard" is losing its ferocity: the crossing from Spiller to Virginia canyon is the least painful yet.

On the Virginia Canyon floor you meet a trail that leads up-canyon to Virginia Pass and Summit Pass, on the Park's border. Across Return Creek (difficult in early season, or even mid season) you spy several adequate campsites and turn south. This gentle descent along Return Creek passes the stream's beautiful bedrock-granite cascades. Dropping into deep, clear potholes, the creek has carved and sculpted the bedrock into smooth, mollescent lines that invite the traveler to run his hands across them. Columbines clustered amid lupine and whorled penstemon add color to the green mats of swamp onion and gooseberry. Quickly you reach and ford smaller McCabe Creek, which may be your last water before Glen Aulin in late season.

Now we begin what will be the *last* climb of major consequence on the Tahoe-Yosemite Trail. On it, some moderately steep switchbacks rise through red fir, hemlock, and pine. Many of the firs have achieved a diameter of 4 feet, and such growth has almost obliterated the **T** blazes that indicate old Cavalry patrol routes. The forest-sheltered switchbacks terminate at the McCabe Lake Trail junction, where our route bears right and descends gently over a duff surface. Birdlife abounds through the moderate-to-dense forest cover of fir and pine, and the hiker is very likely to see chicadees, juncos, warblers, flycatchers, woodpeckers, bluebirds, robins or evening grosbeaks in these precincts.

A short 3/4 mile beyond the last junction, close under Point 9186, you may find water even in late season. Then your route declines gently through cool, moist forest to a fairly large meadow east of Elbow Hill. After threading a course through a few stands of pines, you emerge in an even larger

Return Creek

meadow–about 2 miles long, although the trail does not trace all 2 miles of it. At a stream fork shortly beyond a *very* large boulder to your west, you may find water even in late season. Then the trail climbs over a saddle in a low, forested ridge and gently descends for about ½ mile. Over the next mile, always near Cold Canyon creek, the level, rutted path passes many possible campsites in pleasant meadowy areas studded with small lodgepole pines.

From this camping region a series of easy switchbacks accomplish about half the descent to the Tuolumne River, and where the trail re-reaches the creek there is another good campsite. On the final rocky downhill mile to the river, you catch glimpses of Tuolumne Falls and White Cascade, and their roar carries all the way across the canyon.

Finally, you reach "civilization" at the Glen Aulin High Sierra Camp. Within sight of the camp you pass the Tuolumne River Trail westbound, and in 15 yards come to the little spur trail that crosses Conness Creek on a bridge to the camp. Very meager supplies are sometimes available here. The backpacker campsites just upstream from the "lodge" are very popular

The glen at Glen Aulin

Jeff Schaffer

see MAP 20 see MAP 21

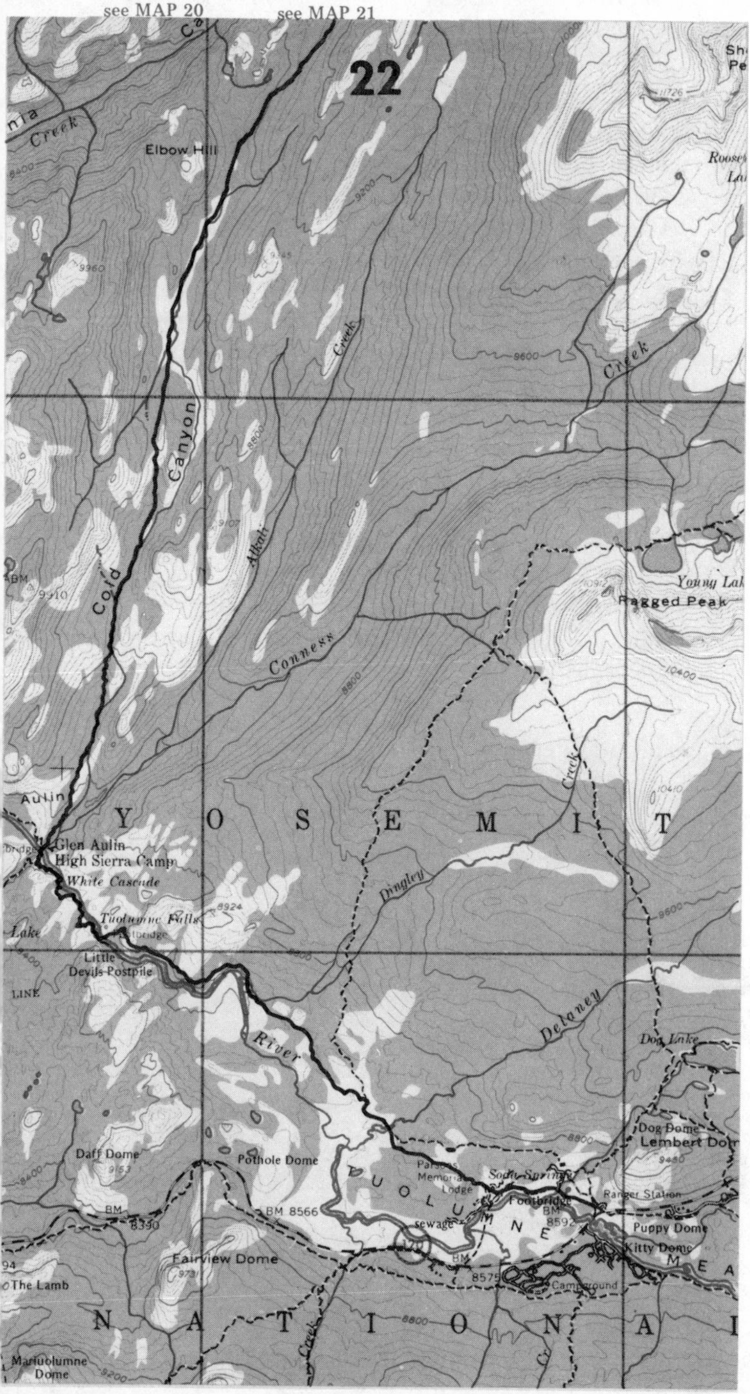

with bears, and you would be less likely to have ursine visitors at one of the campsites a mile or two before you reach Glen Aulin—though it would be no guarantee.

From Glen Aulin the trail crosses the Tuolumne River on a low steel bridge, from which one has excellent views of White Cascade and the deep green pool below it. In a few minutes we reach the May Lake Trail, ascending west, and continue our steep climb to gain the height of White Cascade and Tuolumne Falls. The trail passes a fine viewpoint below the falls, and if the light is right, you'll get a great photograph. Above the falls, the river flows down a series of sparkling rapids separated by large pools and wide sheets of clear water spread out over slightly inclined granite slopes. I always stop here for at least a moment, for I think it one of the most beautiful places on the whole Tahoe-Yosemite Trail.

Soon the trail crosses the river for the last time, on a boulders-and-steel bridge, and then climbs a little way above the gorge the river has cut here. Across the stream one can

Nearing trail's end

easily make out basaltic "Little Devils Postpile," the only volcanic formation anywhere around here. Then we descend to larger, polished slabs near the river, and follow a somewhat ducked route across them for about a mile beside the beckoning waters. When trail tread resumes, we soon cross the three branches of Dingley Creek, which may be dry in late season, and stroll along a "levee" built to raise the trailbed above the flood level here. About ½ mile of almost level walking in cool forest brings the long-distance trekker to the Young Lakes Trail junction, and then he touches the northwest edge of his destination, Tuolumne Meadows. Soon after, we cross three branches of Delaney Creek, the last being the only one of consequence. Just beyond this ford, a trail veers left, bound for the Tuolumne Meadows Stables. We instead veer right and ascend a long, dry, sandy ridge. From the tiny reeded lakes on top of this ridge, the trail drops gently down through meadowed pockets and stands of lodgepole pine to Soda Springs, once a drive-in and then a walk-in campground, but since 1976 closed to camping.

From the effervescent springs, in their dilapidated enclosure, the Tahoe-Yosemite Trail follows a closed-off dirt road east above the north edge of Tuolumne Meadows, the largest subalpine meadow in the Sierra Nevada. The spiring summits of the Cathedral Range across the meadow provide challenging vistas as we stroll the last, level 3/4 mile to a parking lot beside State Highway 120, the Tioga Road.

Beginning by a highway at Meeks Bay and ending by another in Yosemite National Park, our trail has taken us 186 miles over and through some of the Sierra's best attractions. If you have enjoyed meeting the challenge of the Tahoe-Yosemite Trail, you can at this point begin a 188-mile walk through the *high* High Sierra, all the way to the top of Mt. Whitney—for you have been on the famous John Muir Trail since Soda Springs, 3/4 mile back.

PROFILES

The trail profiles on the following pages will help the hiker in his planning. With a pack of about 1/5 your body weight, you can expect to cover two horizontal miles per hour if you are in "ordinary" shape. Add one hour for each 1000 feet of elevation gain. Thus, if you are going 12 miles, and the total of the "ups" is 1500 feet, you can expect to be walking for about: 6 hours + 1.5 hours = 7½ hours. This includes "normal" rest stops.

For downhill walking, use the figure of two miles per hour except where the trail is steep. A steep section will require an extra hour for 2000 feet of descent.

If you are walking without a pack, or you are in really excellent condition, you can do better–perhaps up to 50% better.

If you are walking cross country, it may take you all day to go even 2 miles. There is wide variation, depending on the slope, the footing, the ground cover, and your condition.

The Tahoe-Yosemite Trail is represented in the following pages in 10-mile segments, on a scale with a vertical exaggeration of 520%. In other words, slopes are 5.2 times as steep as the real slopes represented. Nevertheless, the steepness of the slopes on these profiles is related to how you feel when you have to carry a pack up them. The "distance in miles" caption refers to the distance, walking south, from Highway 89 to Meeks Bay.

Not every creek label refers to a creek crossing. For example, the first "Summit City Creek" refers to your arrival beside the stream.

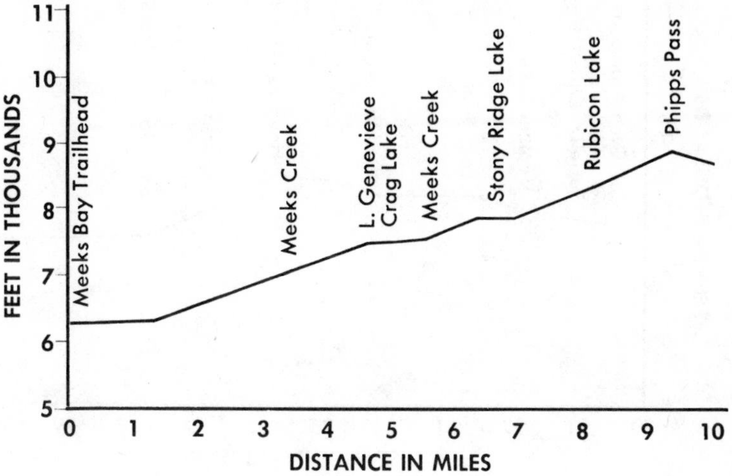
FEET IN THOUSANDS
DISTANCE IN MILES
Meeks Bay Trailhead
Meeks Creek
L. Genevieve
Crag Lake
Meeks Creek
Stony Ridge Lake
Rubicon Lake
Phipps Pass
5
6
7
8
9
10
11
0
1
2
3
4
5
6
7
8
9
10

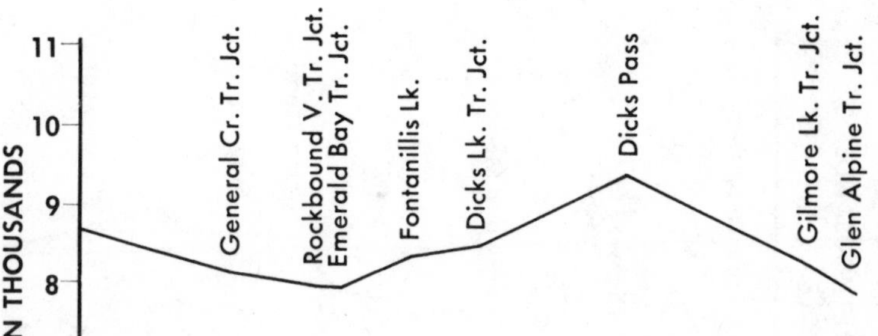
FEET IN THOUSANDS
DISTANCE IN MILES
General Cr. Tr. Jct.
Rockbound V. Tr. Jct.
Emerald Bay Tr. Jct.
Fontanillis Lk.
Dicks Lk. Tr. Jct.
Dicks Pass
Gilmore Lk. Tr. Jct.
Glen Alpine Tr. Jct.
5
6
7
8
9
10
11
10
11
12
13
14
15
16
17
18
19
20

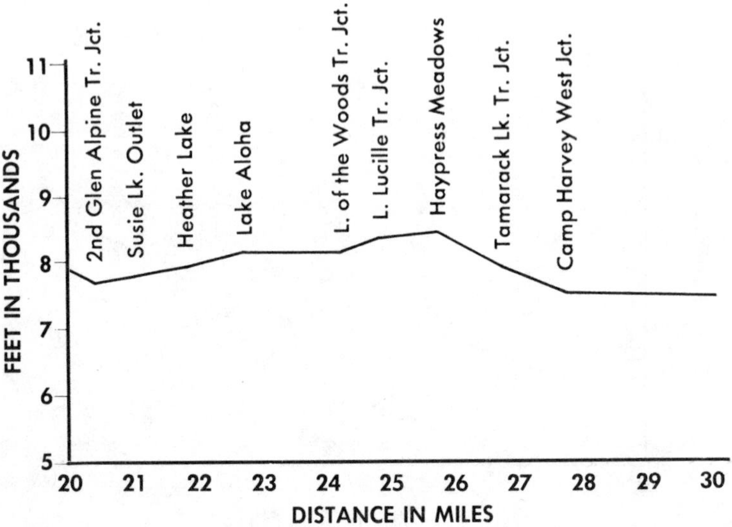
2nd Glen Alpine Tr. Jct.
Susie Lk. Outlet
Heather Lake
Lake Aloha
L. of the Woods Tr. Jct.
L. Lucille Tr. Jct.
Haypress Meadows
Tamarack Lk. Tr. Jct.
Camp Harvey West Jct.
FEET IN THOUSANDS
11
10
9
8
7
6
5
20
21
22
23
24
25
26
27
28
29
30
DISTANCE IN MILES

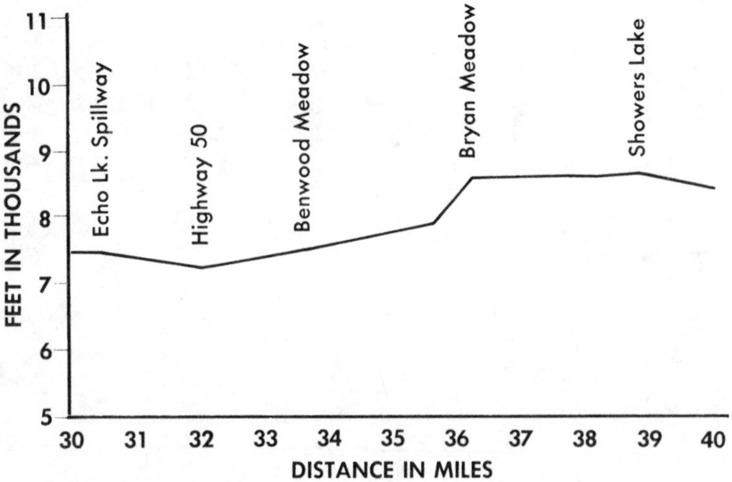
Echo Lk. Spillway
Highway 50
Benwood Meadow
Bryan Meadow
Showers Lake
FEET IN THOUSANDS
11
10
9
8
7
6
5
30
31
32
33
34
35
36
37
38
39
40
DISTANCE IN MILES

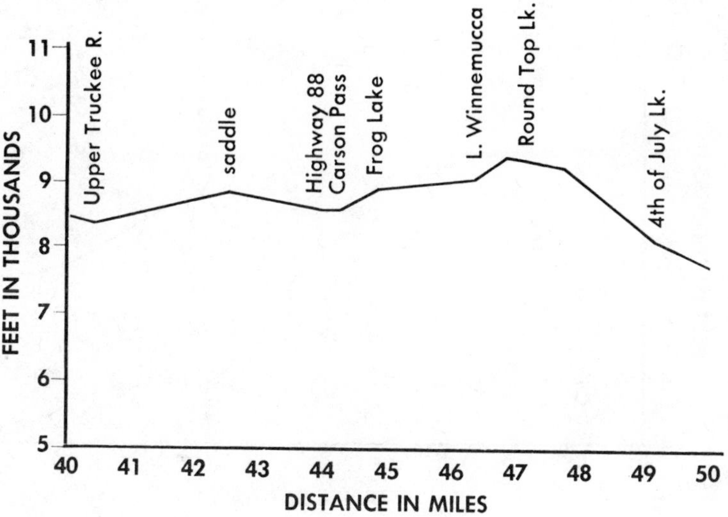
FEET IN THOUSANDS
11
10
9
8
7
6
5
Upper Truckee R.
saddle
Highway 88
Carson Pass
Frog Lake
L. Winnemucca
Round Top Lk.
4th of July Lk.
40
41
42
43
44
45
46
47
48
49
50
DISTANCE IN MILES

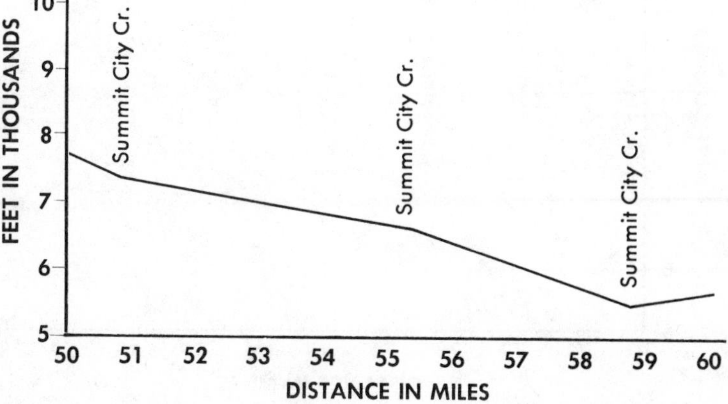
FEET IN THOUSANDS
11
10
9
8
7
6
5
Summit City Cr.
Summit City Cr.
Summit City Cr.
50
51
52
53
54
55
56
57
58
59
60
DISTANCE IN MILES

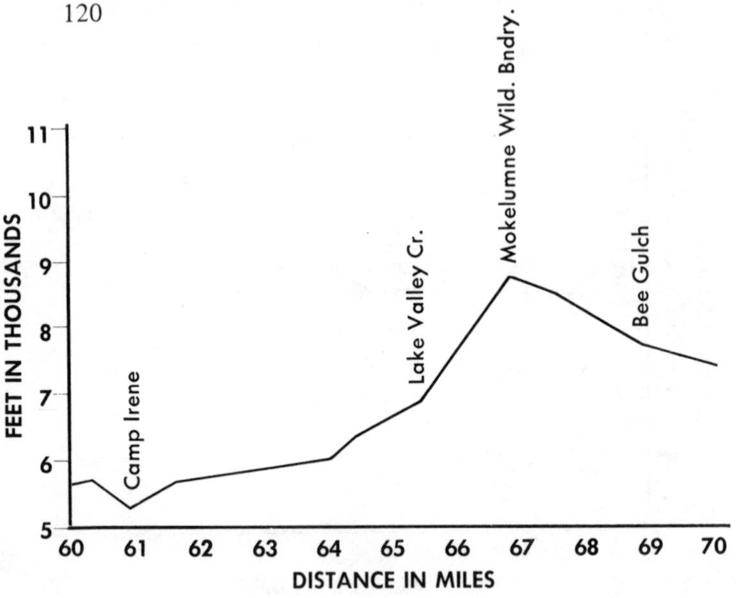
Mokelumne Wild. Bndry.
Lake Valley Cr.
Bee Gulch
Camp Irene
FEET IN THOUSANDS
11
10
9
8
7
6
5
60
61
62
63
64
65
66
67
68
69
70
DISTANCE IN MILES

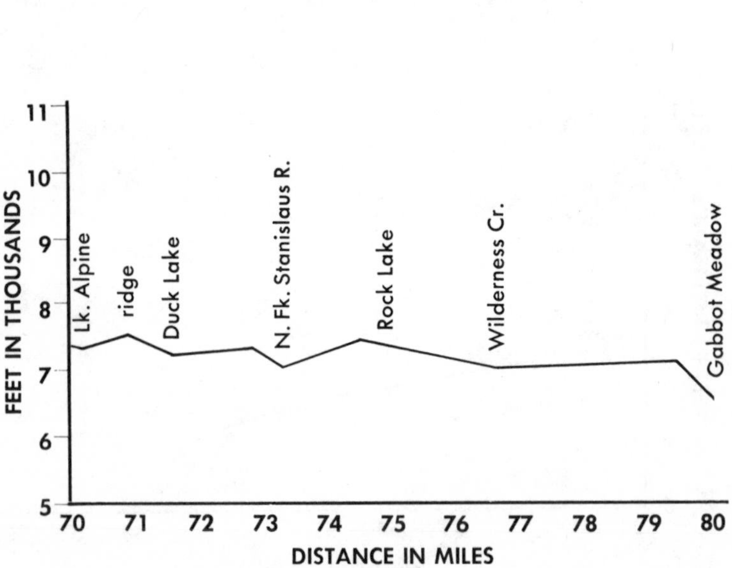
N. Fk. Stanislaus R.
Wilderness Cr.
Gabbot Meadow
Lk. Alpine
ridge
Duck Lake
Rock Lake
FEET IN THOUSANDS
11
10
9
8
7
6
5
70
71
72
73
74
75
76
77
78
79
80
DISTANCE IN MILES

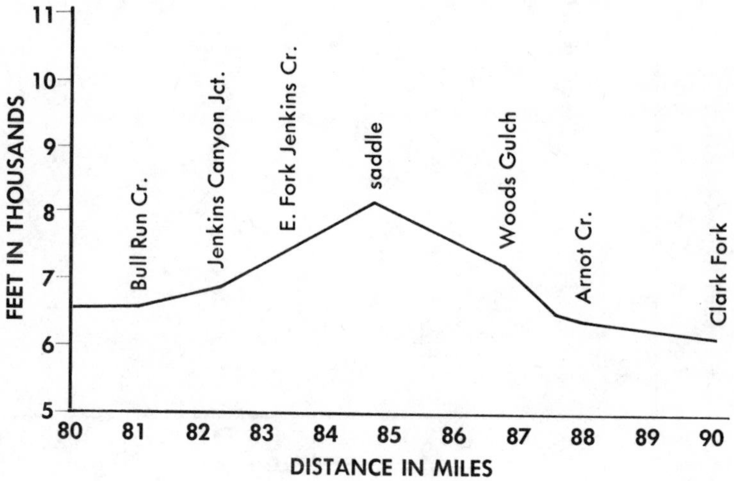
FEET IN THOUSANDS
11
10
9
8
7
6
5
Bull Run Cr.
Jenkins Canyon Jct.
E. Fork Jenkins Cr.
saddle
Woods Gulch
Arnot Cr.
Clark Fork
80
81
82
83
84
85
86
87
88
89
90
DISTANCE IN MILES

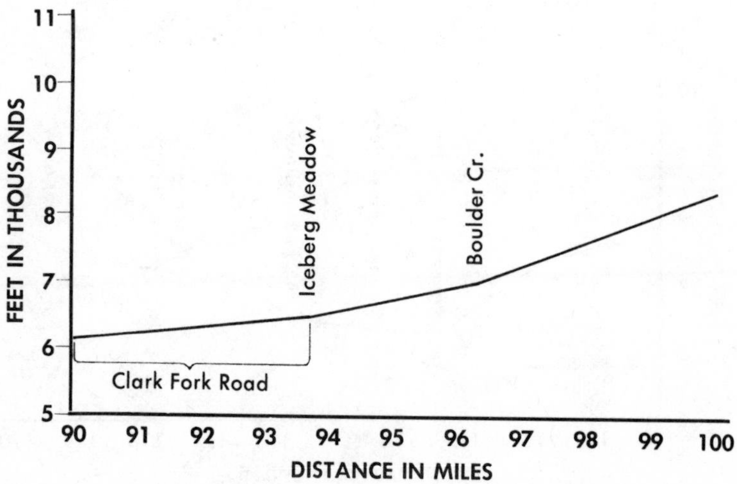
FEET IN THOUSANDS
11
10
9
8
7
6
5
Iceberg Meadow
Boulder Cr.
Clark Fork Road
90
91
92
93
94
95
96
97
98
99
100
DISTANCE IN MILES

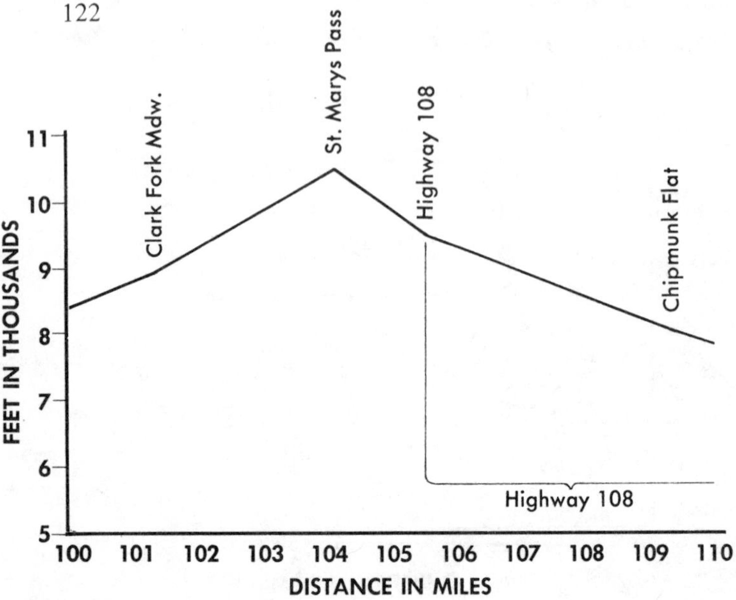
Clark Fork Mdw.
St. Marys Pass
Highway 108
Chipmunk Flat
FEET IN THOUSANDS
11
10
9
8
7
6
5
Highway 108
100
101
102
103
104
105
106
107
108
109
110
DISTANCE IN MILES

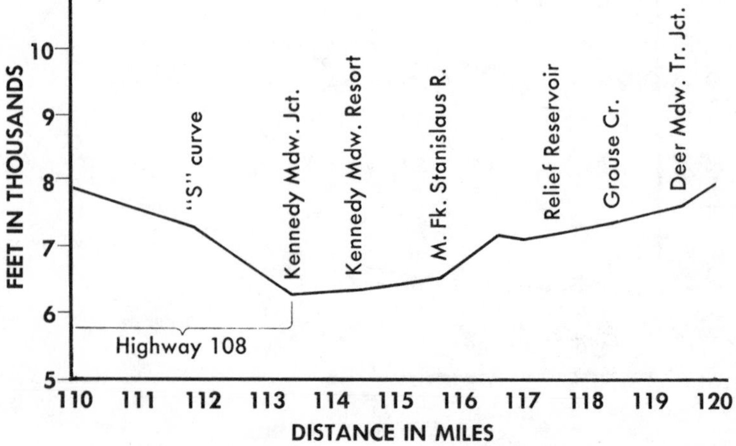
"S" curve
Kennedy Mdw. Jct.
Kennedy Mdw. Resort
M. Fk. Stanislaus R.
Relief Reservoir
Grouse Cr.
Deer Mdw. Tr. Jct.
FEET IN THOUSANDS
11
10
9
8
7
6
5
Highway 108
110
111
112
113
114
115
116
117
118
119
120
DISTANCE IN MILES

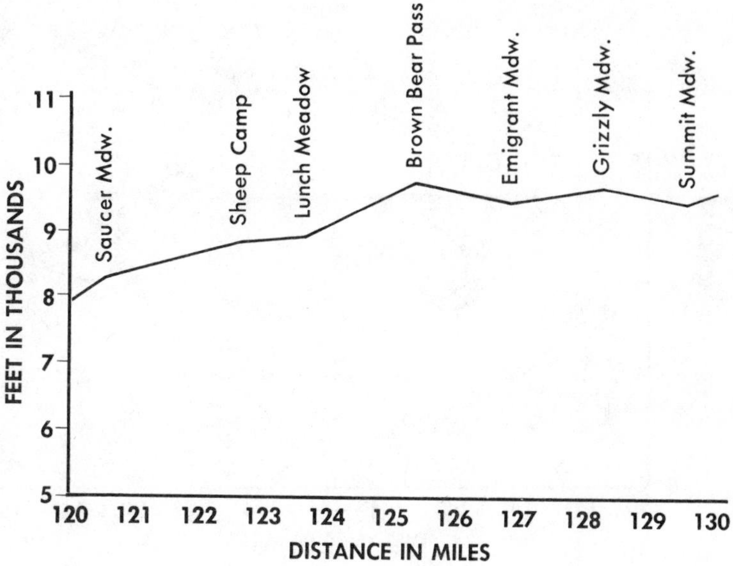

FEET IN THOUSANDS
11
10
9
8
7
6
5
120
121
122
123
124
125
126
127
128
129
130
DISTANCE IN MILES
Saucer Mdw.
Sheep Camp
Lunch Meadow
Brown Bear Pass
Emigrant Mdw.
Grizzly Mdw.
Summit Mdw.

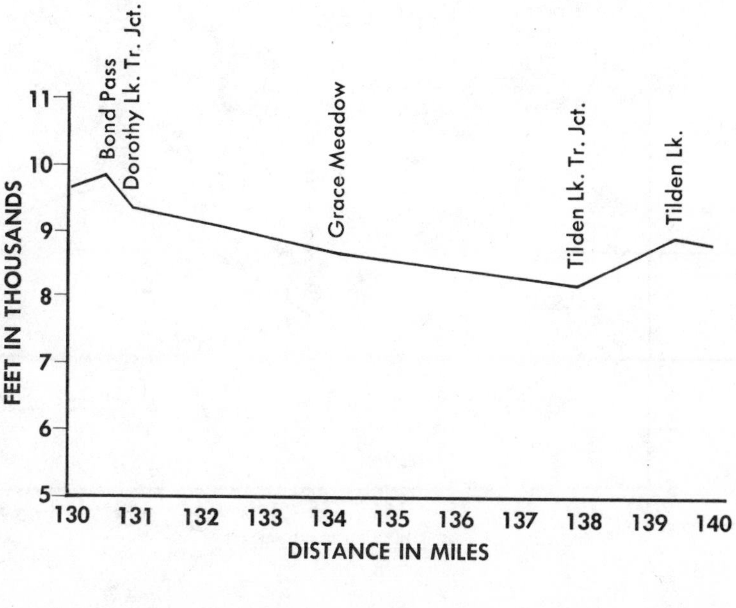

FEET IN THOUSANDS
11
10
9
8
7
6
5
130
131
132
133
134
135
136
137
138
139
140
DISTANCE IN MILES
Bond Pass
Dorothy Lk. Tr. Jct.
Grace Meadow
Tilden Lk. Tr. Jct.
Tilden Lk.

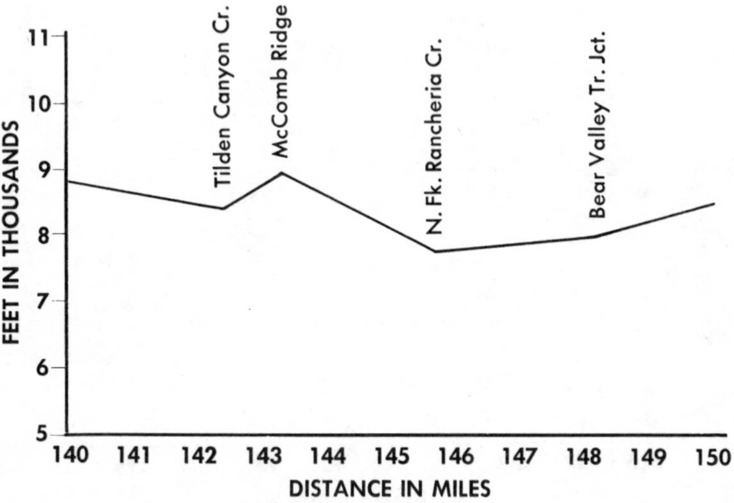
Tilden Canyon Cr.
McComb Ridge
N. Fk. Rancheria Cr.
Bear Valley Tr. Jct.
FEET IN THOUSANDS
11
10
9
8
7
6
5
140
141
142
143
144
145
146
147
148
149
150
DISTANCE IN MILES

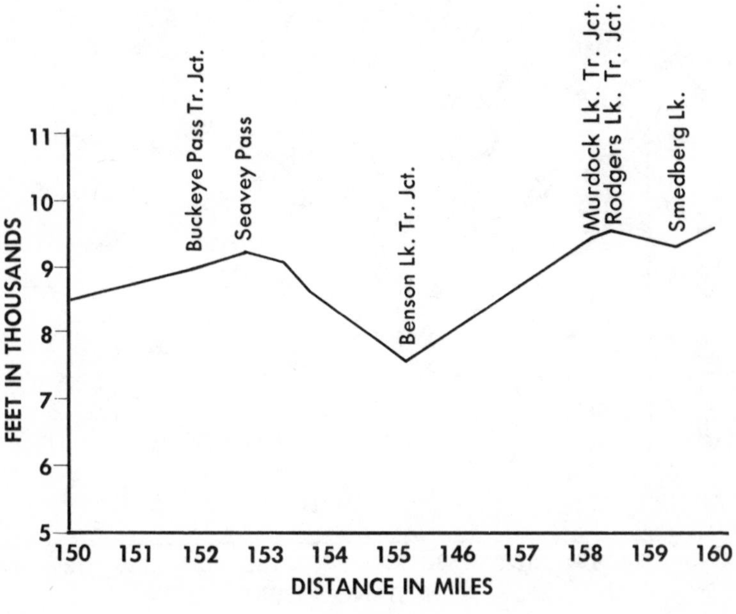
Buckeye Pass Tr. Jct.
Seavey Pass
Benson Lk. Tr. Jct.
Murdock Lk. Tr. Jct.
Rodgers Lk. Tr. Jct.
Smedberg Lk.
FEET IN THOUSANDS
11
10
9
8
7
6
5
150
151
152
153
154
155
146
157
158
159
160
DISTANCE IN MILES

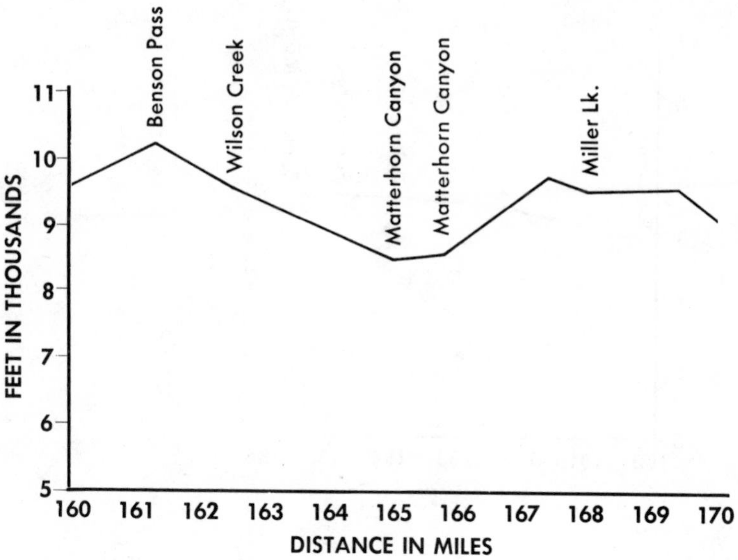
Benson Pass
Wilson Creek
Matterhorn Canyon
Matterhorn Canyon
Miller Lk.
FEET IN THOUSANDS
11
10
9
8
7
6
5
160
161
162
163
164
165
166
167
168
169
170
DISTANCE IN MILES

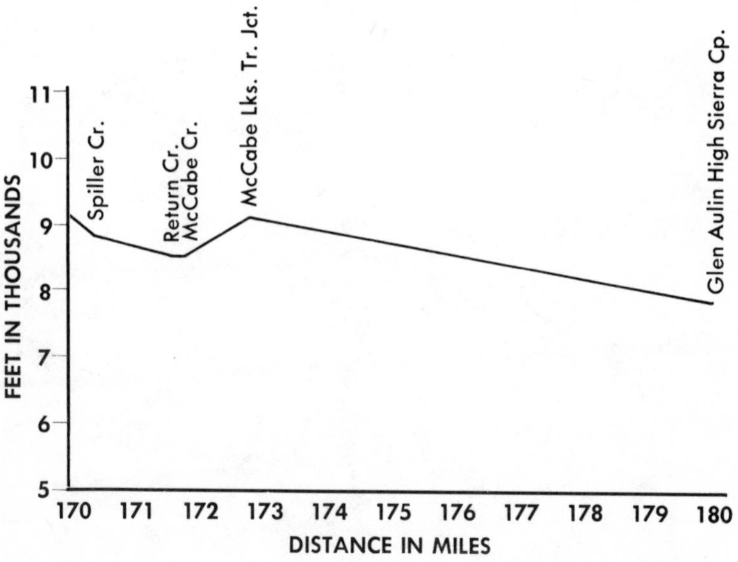
Spiller Cr.
Return Cr.
McCabe Cr.
McCabe Lks. Tr. Jct.
Glen Aulin High Sierra Cp.
FEET IN THOUSANDS
11
10
9
8
7
6
5
170
171
172
173
174
175
176
177
178
179
180
DISTANCE IN MILES

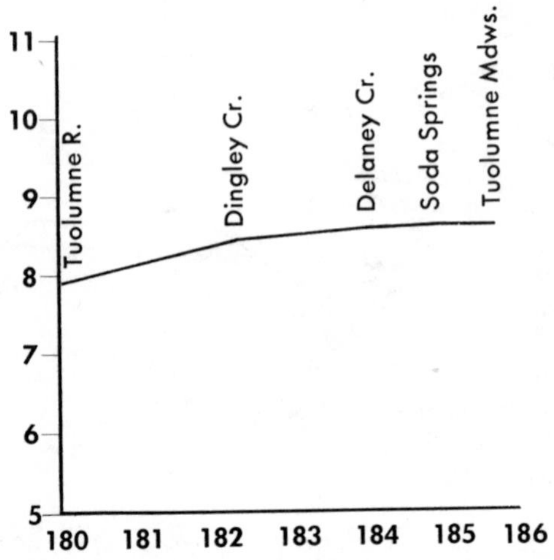
Tuolumne R.
Dingley Cr.
Delaney Cr.
Soda Springs
Tuolumne Mdws.
11
10
9
8
7
6
5
180
181
182
183
184
185
186

BIBLIOGRAPHY

Books

Clarke, Clinton C., *The Pacific Crest Trailway.* Pasadena: The Pacific Crest Trail System Conference, 1945 (out of print)

Farquhar, Francis, *History of the Sierra Nevada.* Berkeley: University of California Press, 1965

Ingles, Lloyd G., *Mammals of the Pacific States.* Stanford, California: Stanford University Press, 1965

Munz, Philip, *California Mountain Wildflowers.* Berkeley: University of California Press, 1963.

Murie, Olaus, *Field Guide to Animal Tracks.* Boston: Houghton, 1958.

Niehaus, Theodore, *Sierra Wildflowers.* Berkeley: University of California Press, 1974.

Peterson, Roger, *A Field Guide to Western Birds.* Boston: Houghton, 1968

Storer, Tracy, and Robert Usinger, *Sierra Nevada Natural History.* Berkeley: University of California Press, 1963

Sudworth, George, *Forest Trees of the Pacific Slope.* New York: Dover Publications, 1967

Pamphlets

Hood, Mary and Bill, *Wildflowers of Yosemite.* Yosemite: Flying Spur Press, 1969

Yosemite Natural History Association
Fishes of Yosemite
Cone-Bearing Trees of Yosemite National Park
Wildflowers of the Sierra
Mammals of Yosemite National Park
Birds of Yosemite

Other Wilderness Press Publications

Schaffer, Jeffrey P. *et al., The Pacific Crest Trail, Volume 1: California,* 1977

Schaffer, Jeffrey P., *The Tahoe Sierra,* revised edition, 1979

Schaffer, Jeffrey P. and Thomas Winnett, *Tuolumne Meadows,* 1977

Winnett, Thomas, *Sierra North, 100 Backcountry Trips in California's Sierra,* 1976

Addresses of U.S. Forest Service and Park Service units along the Tahoe-Yosemite Trail:

Supervisor, Eldorado National Forest
100 Forni Road
Placerville, CA 95667

Supervisor, Stanislaus National Forest
175 S. Fairview Lane
Sonora, CA 95370

Superintendent, Yosemite National Park
Yosemite National Park, CA 95389

Lake Valley District Ranger
Eldorado National Forest
Meyers, CA 95731

Amador District Ranger
Eldorado National Forest
Jackson, CA 95642

Calaveras District Ranger
Stanislaus National Forest
Arnold, CA 95223

Summit District Ranger
Stanislaus National Forest
Pinecrest, CA 95364

Chief Forester, California Region
U.S. Forest Service
630 Sansome St.
San Francisco, CA 94111

(for topographic maps)
Geological Survey
Federal Center
Denver, CO 80225

INDEX